Social Media
Rock Star

Social Media Marketing for Entrepreneurs and Business

GARY BIZZO

Copyright © 2017 Gary Bizzo All rights reserved.

No part of this publication may be reproduced, distributed, or transmitted in any form or by any means, including photocopying, recording, or other electronic or mechanical methods, without the prior written permission of the publisher, except in the case of brief quotations embodied in reviews and certain other non-commercial uses permitted by copyright law.

BizPublishing
(a subsidiary of the Bizzo Management Group Inc.)

ISBN: 978-1974619153

Dedication

I want to dedicate this book to my wife, Jo Ann. She's the glue that holds me together and is the best partner a man can have. She always believes in me and supports me in so many ways. It's one more example she gives me every day of her unconditional love. Thanks Baby!

4

Table of Contents

Acknowledgments 9
Foreword 11
Introduction 13
Chapter 1 – Social Media, the New Singularity? 21
Chapter 2 – An Industry Overview 25
   Is Social Media Simplifying or Complicating Business? 25
   Social Media Platforms by the Numbers 38
   What Are Brand Influencers? 39
Chapter 3 – Planning Your Social Media 41
   What Social Media Platform to Use for Your Business 43
   Your Social Media Profiles 57
   Who Does Social Media Well? 58
   Your Social Media Action Plan 59
   A SWOT Analysis 62
Chapter 4 – Working with the Four Generations 65
   What Are the Generations and How to Market to Each 66
     The Top Content Forms All Generations Like: 72
     The Bottom Content Forms All Generations Like: 72
   Specific Content for Each Generation 72
     What Generations Like the Most 73
Chapter 5 – A Basic Checklist for SM Engagement 75
Chapter 6 – A Lot More About Twitter 97
   Your Twitter Content 103
   Your Goals 105
Chapter 7 – Creating & Adding Value 109
   Telling a Story 110
   Share Your Expertise 111
   Answer Questions 112
   Discussions 112
   Sharing Tips or Hints 113
   Behind the Scenes 114
   Sharing Deals with Customers (or potentials) 115
   Pay It Forward 116
   Solving a Problem 117

Chapter 8 – 30 Ways to Use Social Media for Business 119
1. Get Feedback 120
2. Create Demand 121
3. Offer Discounts 121
4. Get Attention 122
5. Spread the Word 123
6. Build Brand Loyalty 124
7. Establish a Community 124
8. Answer Questions 125
9. Provide Support 126
10. Get Clients 127
11. Improve CRM 127
12. Empower Staff 129
13. Monitor Trends 129
14. Identify Influencers 130
15. Reach Out 130
16. Discuss Features 131
17. Facilitate Testing 132
18. Debunk Myths 132
19. Market Offerings 133
20. Forge Relationships 134
21. Develop Authority 134
22. Build Links 135
23. Raise Funds 135
24. Get Publicity 136
25. Watch the Competition 137
26. Find Talent 137
27. Organize 138
28. Create Value 139
29. Locate Markets 140
30. Meet Peers 140

Chapter 9 – Social Media's Return on Investment (ROI) 143
10 Value-added ROI's from Social Media 144
1. Your Reputation 144
2. Reducing Risk 145
3. Customer Retention 146
4. Finding Suppliers 147
5. Public Exposure 147
6. Brand Association 148

7. Immediate Revenue 148
  8. Long Term Revenue 149
  9. Business Intelligence 149
  10. Differentiation 150

Chapter 10 – Social Media Tools for Small Business 151
  Dashboards / Management Tools 152
  Social Media Analytics Tools 160
  Visual Content Tools 166
  Social Media Monitoring Tools 170
  Social Media Content Tools 171
  Miscellaneous Tools 174

Chapter 11 – Raise Your Game in SM Marketing 183
  Outbound Marketing (Push Marketing) 183
  Inbound vs. Outbound 185
  Inbound Marketing (Pull Marketing) 187
  How Can You Use the Benefits of Inbound Marketing? 190
  Challenges 195
  Opportunities 197

Chapter 12 – The Power of SM (& SM Horror Stories) 201
Chapter 13 – A Twitter Social Media Case Study 209
Chapter 14 – Conclusion 217
Special Offer 223
Appendix 224
  6-Step Social Media Checklist For Everyone 224
  Social Media Tools for Business 227
About the Author 231
  Need Help Implementing Your Social Media? 232

"A brand is no longer what we tell the consumer it is – it is what consumers tell each other it is"

Scott Cook
Cofounder of Intuit

Acknowledgments

No one can achieve any sense of confidence or greatness without the support of great people and a community of like-minded individuals behind them. My friends have always been supportive. Thank you to:

My fab three business incubator client mentors: Gordon Ross, Carl de Jong and Albert Yu. Another mentor Gerardo Lopez, George Moen (serial entrepreneur) and Doug "DA" Anderson (coach extraordinaire). Nick Noorani (author/publisher/mentor), Bob Munro (the ultimate salesman) who always believes I'm the guy to fix anything. Todd Buchanan at Equifaira Advisors the Liquidity Event Planners, who woke me up to a new career in private finance for start-ups.

To the countless others I haven't mentioned but think about every day. You are all winners – thank you for being in my life!

Foreword

When Gary Bizzo asked me to write this forward I felt very honoured. I first met Gary Bizzo over 20 years ago when we were working together mentoring men to become better versions of themselves so that they could be better husbands, fathers and men in their communities. The central concept of this important work is honour so I don't use that word lightly.

Gary extended that work to entrepreneurs and companies as a Certified Business Counsellor (a designation from APEC at Acadia University). He has mentored over one thousand investors, business leaders and new business start-ups.

His avocation is as a social media networker. Bizzo has an international reputation as an 'Agent of Change' using Social Media. He has hundreds of thousands of followers on a range of social media platforms. He believes social media initiatives, including inbound marketing and community engagement, change the fabric of our lives and allows each of us to make a difference.

I now call Gary Bizzo my social media mentor. He makes social media simple for those of us in business who often rely on others for the latest in the fast-moving online information highway. Gary's stories of how he built his following, and why he was recognized by Forbes as a top online global influencer cannot fail to impress. London-based Richtopia said "Bizzo was on the List of the philanthropists and social entrepreneurs top 200 of 2017 as one of the most influential leaders in the World".

In short, Gary ensures that being a *Social Media Rockstar* need not be a mystery. He made me realize that we can often keep on top of our social media from our phones in minutes a day and it can all be done with honour and integrity. That's why he's my social media mentor.

If you are reading this book, you are on your way to making Gary your mentor too. Smart move!

B. Todd Buchanan

Co-Founder and Managing Partner
EQUIFAIRA
Liquidity Event Planners

Introduction

I wanted to write this book because when I first started my ad agency in the '90's companies had to pay through the nose to advertise. Billboards, brochures, pamphlets, mail-outs on postal routes, television, radio and newspaper or magazines were the standard form of getting the word out. The sales guy at the magazine would tell me "you realize you have to run this ad for at least six times before someone will remember your name enough to buy it, right". Shut your cake hole!

Companies became big only if they had the thousands to spend on all these forms of advertising. Guerrilla marketing has supplanted the old marketing schemes and a simple well-thought out social media plan can devastate those old campaigns yet the cost is pennies versus thousands of dollars.

Direct mail was replaced by email, faxes were just dumped but turned into emails. The hours of networking we did away from our families became Facebook or, for me, LinkedIn, Television became YouTube which is fine with me, radio was replaced by the podcast (which I have started) and newspapers are trying to stay afloat but have been replaced by blogs. I guess the good old billboard still is there and probably does an effective job, but for the money I'd rather stick to free or near free marketing strategies using social media.

I guess I am what people call a serial entrepreneur. I've had so many businesses one of my close friends, Rick Dennis, showed me a business card box, the kind you get 250 business cards from the printer. Inside were all my business cards I had given him over the years and it almost filled the box. From my days as a record promoter and American Federation of Musicians booking agent to my commercial photography business and those two years when I was an arms dealer in the 1980's. If only I had made a million on each company!

I came to Vancouver in 1974, right out of the University of

New Brunswick on the East Coast. I came for a record company convention figuring my experience paying my way through university by booking rock bands might get me a job in the big city.

I did, but it was tough, working nights and constantly selling bands to club owners. One competitor also selling rock bands in Vancouver kept trying to get me to quit the guy who gave me the break in Vancouver and come to work for him. The fancy cars and big money were very tempting.

I went back home to New Brunswick at Christmas time to get married and soon began thinking of my future and what would be best for 'us'. I wrote a letter (yes it was before email) to the competitor and told him I was unhappy where I was working and I would be glad to take his offer of the big time job.

I heard nothing and figured it was the holidays and maybe I'd hear back from him when I got back to work. When I got into my office the boss was very upset with me. The competitor had photocopied my letter, pasted it on his office waiting room wall and had sent the original to my boss. Needless to say I had to find another job!

All this time I was taking pictures of everything I could and started a small photography business that clearly was not going to support my wife and I. The lack of confidence was a major problem but I figured it could be a second income somewhere down the road.

I had studied Behavior Modification and Criminology in university so soon got a job as a Parole Officer for the federal government. I loved the excitement, the danger (I was held hostage 3 times) and the pay. However, my little photography business was growing and I was getting stressed. No one had ever heard of burnout but I was seriously there after seven years fighting the bad guys.

My career in the government ended on a Tuesday and there was no love lost between my bosses and I when I left. It was that Tuesday that I decided I was going to be in charge of my life from then on. That first unemployed night was scary until my best friend called me and said, "I have been waiting for you to leave that miserable job so I could ask you to be my partner in my company, Brenlee Aircraft Corporation".

We started selling small airplanes as my bud was an accomplished jet pilot. We then moved into selling bigger planes like 747's, then oil refineries and finally got into the lucrative arms business. All the same people were involved in all three so it was a normal progression. Yeah, I know, that's a very unsavory business. Back in the 1980's, Adnan Kasogi, the world's largest arms dealer had been named Time Magazine's Man of the Year. It was legitimate and we were licensed from all the government departments in Canada.

It too was tough because the buyers of arms were skeptical that a couple of 30 year old guys from Vancouver could sell them Kalashnikovs (AK-47's) and Uzi submachine guns or US surface-to-air missiles. We could and much more!

It became a case of running out of money trying to close the big deals and a whole lot of scary characters. So I went the safe route and with renewed confidence opened my first photography studio and put the shingle on the door...and waited and waited for customers.

The customers eventually did come and I went from doing just photography to print production (brochure, annual reports, advertising pieces) to web development to a full boutique ad agency.

The people I was meeting as an ad agency were CEO's and the excitement of deals and more deals lured me into many ventures. You just start to hang with different people and opportunities are always around if you look hard enough. Unfortunately I didn't have Warren Buffet's advice of look at hundreds of deals and pick the best one. I tended to get involved in all kinds of deals, throw them against the wall to see which one stuck.

I had photographed 27 world leaders, Presidents (Clinton of the US, Boris Yeltsin, Russia) and Kings (well, Prince Charles and others), attended a Summit for APEC, covered rock concerts and hung out with rock stars (Bee Gees, Joe Cocker, Tina Turner), worked on political elections and covered events for national magazines. So I figured I had 'been there and done that!

I eventually lost my passion for my beloved photography and after incredible milestones said – next? I took two years off.

For some reason I had applied for a job and was called for an interview six months after I had applied but had forgotten what the job was for. So in the middle of the interview I asked. The interviewers thought I was nuts but offered me the position of running a business incubator since I was a project manager of sorts when I ran my ad agency.

Not really wanting a job must have given me a bit of arrogance that they liked and they offered me the 'job'. I told them that if I was to work with entrepreneurs I had to remain one myself so they gave me incredible leeway in running the most successful business incubator in the country in the

1990's. I stayed 10 years. It gave me incredible insights into business, allowed me to pursue a Certification in Business Counseling from Acadia University and start my MBA. It also gave me unbelievable connections in both the business world and government. It also got me involved in marketing using social media. It was an obvious progression for me because marketing, as we knew it, was changing and it wasn't waiting for anyone.

While running the incubator I published my first book, "How to Start a Successful Business – the First Time" on Amazon. It was a critical success and gave me a forum to be heard while giving me some very lucrative keynote speaking engagements. It also made me realize that people enjoyed my writing and I ended up writing for local, national and international magazines. All the while using my array of social media tools to cross promote.

Being heavily involved in social media, I realized I loved the engagement I got on a daily basis from people all over the world. I became good at it, I guess, because I had a great passion for it and started referring to it as my avocation. They say if you work at something long and hard enough you become a local, then national then international expert.

I want you to know that I don't think I am better at this than you, if anything, I am more like you than you can imagine, it's just that all the 'stuff' in this book are things that I have used, mainly by trial and error and I found that they worked.

As Russell Brunson said in his book '*DOTCOM Secrets*' all of his strategies for having better web traffic and conversions are 'evergreen', meaning that the content is timeless. In this social media landscape, that is a pretty bold statement so "I will say that mine is evergreen as well minus some of the suggested apps that I recommend. It's been a challenge to keep them up to date as some close, some are bought up and some are replaced by better ones; so bear with me and I hope you enjoy my material.

I arrived at the point where I know that my experience in social media can help any business and when other people from around the world tell you that you are global influencer you have to believe it.

With every business I have owned I didn't measure success by how much money I made. My yardstick was; am I having fun?

I am having a ball!

Chapter 1 – Social Media, the New Singularity?

I remember getting into social media in 1993, specifically as a web developer in a brand new medium called the World Wide Web or the Internet. In 1992 an estimate for all sales on the Internet for the year 1993 were estimated 'conservatively' to be about 2 million dollars. I heard, last year, that Alibaba did 2 billion dollars in sales in one weekend. Wow! Talk about scalability.

The information highway, as it was originally called, has now taken a different turn. It's taken us everywhere to the point where more than 1/3 of the world is connected to each other. If you look at it that way futurist Ray Kurzweil's theory that the Internet has created a singularity is true. Kurzweil took

Marshall McLuhan's 'the medium is the message' in the 1970's and updated it.

The idea of a singularity means that the world is now connected in a global consciousness. Social Media has evolved to transcend geopolitical boundaries and the usual social constructs. Engagement is the new word to describe interaction between people, groups and ideas online.

> *"The term singularity describes the moment when a civilization changes so much that its rules and technologies are incomprehensible to previous generations. Think of it as a point-of-no-return in history."*
> - Annalee Newitz, American Journalist

Kurzweil felt that information technologies would advance so far and so fast that they would enable mankind to transcend our biological limitations. Technology may have given us the tools but social media has given us the content and will to make mankind leap past the futurists' observations.

Back in the 1970's people felt that Artificial Intelligence would 'take over the world', if not, redefine how we work and live in it. In the 1990's people started thinking that the Internet would make the leap over Artificial Intelligences as the leading method of change but the concept simply overtook us without even being aware. I remember noticing changes to the way I saw the world when cell phones became Smartphones, when people had their face buried in the phone as they walked, played, worked and; from a recent study slept.

Most thinkers thought the singularity would be jump-started by extremely rapid technological and scientific changes. These changes would be so fast, and so profound, that every aspect of our society would be transformed, from our bodies and families to our governments and economies. Can you agree that social media has done that?

Singularities have happened in the past. The industrial revolution (I love the SteamPunk effect) and the Information Age geared us up to accepting massive change defined it globally and much faster. Self-replicating molecular machine, also called autonomous nanotechnology was seen as a singularity. Basically the idea is that if we can build machines that manipulate matter at the atomic level, we can control our world in the most granular way imaginable. I can tell you from experience that nanotechnology will drastically alter the way we live but I think it is social media that pulls us all together into one consciousness. Considering all these dynamic milestones, in my mind social media has become the next visible singularity.

Add memes to this and you can see how viral social media has made change inevitable. A **meme** (/ˈmiːm/ meem) is "an idea, behavior, or style that spreads from person to person within a culture." We can see how viral ideas can spread within a culture easily through word of mouth etc. but with social media can jump the cultural boundaries easily and instantly. Remember how the 'Arab Spring' leaped over its' Egyptian boundaries to excite and incite the world about democracy?

> *"Our evidence suggests that social media carried a cascade of messages about freedom and democracy across North Africa and the Middle East, and helped raise expectations for the success of political uprising,"*
> - Philip Howard, Communications Professor
> University of Washington

A young man told me some time ago that he wasn't on social media because he thought it was stupid 'to tell people what he was eating for breakfast'. I remember those early days but as a singularity, social media has not only allowed us to spread wider but has allowed us to delve into things deeper out of necessity. We are curious beings and it's little wonder why we have our noses buried in our Smartphones too many times in the day.

Are You Engaged? You Better Be!

Chapter 2 – An Industry Overview

Is Social Media Simplifying or Complicating Business?

This book is generally for the entrepreneur but is certainly going to be informative for anyone wanting to increase their profile, become a thought-leader or to learn more about the different options open to you as you navigate the variety of social media platforms.

Social media has created a paradigm shift in terms of how we do business and what tools entrepreneurs can use to market to the consumer. Some may argue that the rise of social media is, in fact, the greatest 'invention' since the computer.

Social media has created a new way of doing business not just in promoting our businesses or us.

Let's discuss defining new strategies to take a business to market, digital branding versus traditional marketing, and the top mediums for social engagement, the benefits and downfalls of social media.

In the 1960's Marshall McLuhan gave us the famous line, "the medium is the message'. In the new millennium, the message is definitely 'the content' and social media tools like Facebook, Twitter and LinkedIn, the medium, have changed the way we not only do business but how we engage with others in our life.

Traditional marketing like flyers, brochure, TV, radio, business cards and static websites have been replaced in recent years by YouTube, social media mega players and a new focus on inbound versus outbound marketing. Outbound, the traditional marketing method relied on the entrepreneur to get his message out to the masses in the hopes the buyer would be swayed by the message they put forth. Billions of dollars are still regularly spent to garner the dollar of the consumer although social media savvy marketers are moving their marketing budgets to social media instead.

Inbound marketing has changed the face of advertising because social media draws people to the entrepreneur and his company with content that the consumer desires and is actively seeking on the Internet. Forrester Research released its 5 year forecast detailing that social media advertising spending in the US is expected to reach $16.2 billion by 2019 up from $7.3 billion in 2014, growing at a five-year compounded annual growth rate of 17.4%. This represents a 10-fold increase from 2009.

Canada's largest sports retailer, SportChek, conducted an experiment in 2015. For 2 weeks the prolific flyer company didn't print a single flyer; rather it converted its marketing to Facebook instead. SportChek's market research had indicated only 17% read their flyers delivered the traditional way through fillers in newspapers. In those 2 weeks the retailer showed a spike of 12% in sales and featured items jumped 23% over the same period last year. Based on these findings they are soon to divert 25% of their annual $20M ad budget to social media. In comparison Canadian Tire spends $100M a year just on flyers. These market giants are still hesitant to divert their entire budgets to digital since consumers find flyers a tough habit to drop. The savings to a small business owner is staggering.

Clearly these numbers are significant and show a shift to the

Internet when one considers that the major benefit of social media marketing is that it is free. The advertising revenues noted indicate traditional markets for large corporations are now shifting their spending patterns to reflect the new delivery methods.

What does social media do for the entrepreneur? It has created a fast and effective channel to build and enhance your brand and reputation. It builds visibility, established brand credibility and can be effective in creating a special type of customer loyalty based on word of mouth engagement.

Does social media make the journey easier for the entrepreneur? It is much like the early days of computers when we all felt computers would reduce the 'paper' in our lives. One could easily say that the rise of social media has made connectivity and engagement easier but has taken over a portion of our lives that in the past has been private. Engagement used to mean meeting other entrepreneurs in a social environment like a tradeshow over drinks. Now it means connecting over the impersonal but far reaching social networks available to us.

Social media is your new Rolodex (ask someone over 50 if you don't know what that is); it's a source for global crowdfunding via Indiegogo and Kickstarter. Imagine financing your business from investors $5 at a time through a global network of like-minded people who see your vision and are happy to invest in your product instantly. I must admit crowdfunding and its' nephew Equity crowdfunding are clever ways to raise money but it's not the easy method one would led you to believe. Unless you have the next SmartWatch or an innovative piece of technology people are hesitant to invest and campaigns that are not mind-blowing will fail using this platform.

Crowdsourcing is the ability to find the right partner for your business as if borders didn't exist. FiveR is a tool that allows you to peruse classifieds of people who will do work for you for five dollars, fast and efficiently. Imagine 10 years ago having your logo designed for five dollars or having your resume reviewed by a professional for five bucks. FiveR has arrived, is effective and is guaranteed.

This trend, offshore crowdsourcing, is happening in business that on the surface seems very logical and cost effective. It's not new but suddenly people believe it is the answer to all their marketing, production and creative business needs.

I've used offshore creative 'agencies' to do work for me. The work is always unbelievably cheap and the turnaround is appealing because if you're using India or China it's 12-13 hours ahead. I give them a job near the end of my workday and it's ready by the next morning – ideal! I'd also say the work is often good if your supplier speaks English very well.

The problem I've found is that they don't always understand everything you say and even with the best-written instructions jobs just don't make the grade. I hired a Pakistani freelancer to do a logo redesign for $15. Astounding you might say but it's not what I wanted. They all say they are happy to redo the work and they do but also in the end the task cannot compare to what I can get from an established agency in metro Vancouver who understands not only what I need but also what I don't even know what I need.

A case in point is I needed two 'explainer' videos, short at only 90 seconds to explain two companies I was working with. Made in Pakistan, the graphics were awesome but didn't get the western flavor I needed. They did have a choice of narrators and I had a sample voice to choose from. I got them so cheaply that I didn't send them back for an edit I just accepted them as is and moved on. I will forever think how the videos could have been better every time my client plays them. He thought they were ok but I was disappointed.

iStockphoto has taken the lucrative copyright incomes of

photographers and reduced them to pennies a photograph by opening up stock libraries to the world. Instead of charging $100 for a one-time use the photographer can sell the same image hundreds of times for a dollar. While the market has changed, the photographer has not lost his livelihood because of commodities of scale.

Virtual offices via Smartphones have replaced the expensive downtown offices with our wireless connection to the world and customers. Business cards are still a source of brand identity but likely include a QR bar code on it somewhere which, when scanned by a Smartphone, can take the viewer directly to a blog, website or special offer on the Internet. Some serious marketers like Canada's Boston Pizza have an app that sends persons signed on to their site updates on job opportunities. Your phone is indeed your Rolodex (that old time product again).

Social media has changed the way we perceive and are perceived personally and for business. It is an agent of change for others. We are familiar with the social media campaign of President Obama who admitted that social media played a major role in his first election. The death of pop icon Michael Jackson was first reported by a Tweet. President Trump actually seems to be running his administration through his Twitter account. That may sound crazy until you realize he has 30M followers (March 2017).

Social media in the form of Foursquare and Yelp allows marketers to use GPS to lure customers to their retail establishment using proximity offers and gamifies the experience so people stay engaged in the hunt for good deals. Retailers, especially, who are not socially aware can easily be left out of reviews, specials and customers.

Of course, we use Facebook to connect with old friends and build new ones, LinkedIn is more of a professional resume for business people and raves that 54% of all job recruiters are followers. This is a good indicator of its relevance to job seekers and employers. Twitter with its incredibly succinct 140 characters is also immediate and subject to viral and trending situations.

Social media has created a situation where everyone can make a difference in the world. Imagine a world where everyone is accountable and anyone can question officials in both government and industry – it is here now. In the early 2000's Diane Urquhart became a major whistleblower for Canadian government fraud but remains insignificant and largely anonymous because her expose happened before social media. We are all aware of the two top whistleblowers cum heroes, Snowden and Wikileaks Julian Assange. They are either called heroes or traitors but however you look at it they saw injustice and sought to expose it to the world. In today's world privacy is one of our most cherished assets.

Social media became the catalyst and the unifying force behind the 'Arab Spring' and other rebellions from the grassroots of society.

I read an article on page 17 of Canada's Globe & Mail newspaper by two journalists about the high salaries and perks paid to NGO charity CEO's like the Salvation Army and Save the Children. I was incensed and began a social media campaign to get the news out using twitter and my blog. Unknown to me CTV picked up my social media feeds and got the interest of a Canadian Member of Parliament. She presented a Private Members Bill to the House of Commons and it passed First Reading. I know the sequence of events because she called me and asked me to present a brief to the House of Commons about my efforts. I did and Bill C-470 went through the legislative process, albeit watered down a little, to make charities more transparent. The bottom line? **One person can make a difference.**

Business and social media provide some interesting statistics. According to Stats Canada, 85% of clients expect companies they buy from to be on social media and 82% trust companies more if they are on social media. In 2003, 22% of people trusted 'people like me'. It give them accountability making them more appealing to the consumer. In 2014 that number has risen to 92% according to Forbes. With the top three social media platforms, Facebook, Google and Twitter garnering almost two billion followers it is unwise for an entrepreneur to ignore social media and its effect on the marketplace.

Canadians have embraced social media ahead of most other industrial states. Some more statistics from Forrester Research indicates, 86% of Canadians are on social media, we average two hours and 19 minutes on social media per day, 89% of us use our Smartphones for local internet searches and 27% of Canadians have made a purchase on their Smartphone in the past year. One would think these numbers alone are compelling for entrepreneurs to embrace and join the social media wave.

We should talk of the different platforms. The website which has been the mainstay of entrepreneurs to get 'the word out' is dead. Its static format where information becomes stale as soon as the site is created is not interesting and once its information is viewed becomes a boring lifeless Internet experience. The Blog format, usually on WordPress, with its changing content has made blogs not only dynamic and changeable but has a built-in ability to add custom pieces that can allow you to gather customer information, build lists, get feedback while providing potential customers with great information which they seek. Customers return often to see what has changed on the site and if they find the information useful they will pass the site on to others via social media or word of mouth.

This free marketing is considered grassroots guerilla tactics. Guerrilla marketing was initially used by small and medium sized businesses, but it is increasingly being adopted by big business. The concept of guerrilla marketing rises from an unconventional system of promotion that relies on patience, energy, and imagination rather than a big advertising budget.

Entrepreneurs are consumed by demographics. Business owners find it a constant battle to find new customers and although social media has given them free tools and access to a wide expanse of potential clients social media is still on the edge of being fully utilized. There is endless data indicating that Twitter has had an increase of 79% since 2012 in baby boomers (those aged 55-64). Baby Boomers still run most of the big corporations and are just a little slow to use social media but they need to be recognized.

Google has shown a slightly lower 56% increase in users 45-54 and Facebook at 46% for the same age bracket. The older generation is now embracing social media like never before and marketers are clearly taking notice with media buys directed at this segment. Gone are the kids who dominated early social media. Youth between 12-17 now account for only 11% of social media users on Twitter.

The delivery of Twitter's tweets is a source of its popularity. With the maximum message size of 140 characters it has always been a challenge to get the message out to reach your customer about your service or product. Gone are the days when 'tweets' consisted of what you had for breakfast. It is now the domain of corporate branding. With Twitter you can 'follow' or reach 1000 new customers a day. Can you visualize reaching that number with Facebook, mail or phone? Large advertisers realize the importance of Twitter to the point that Microsoft, PayPal and 3M have paid me in excess of $300US per tweet. I know it sounds crazy to me too but I'll cash those checks as long as they keep coming to my door.

Social media has changed the face of customer service for entrepreneurs. In the past your reputation was solid as long as you could keep clients happy one at a time. I had a recent issue with Delta Hotels. Bad service led me to complain on social media and with vast numbers of followers behind me I made quite an impact. When the President of Delta Hotels called me on a holiday to assuage my issues I knew I had hit a nerve and he finally understood the impact of social media on customer service and retention.

What does the entrepreneur need to do to keep a positive social media outlook? One needs to have a blog with a 'call to action' (a form to fill in, something for the potential customer to do for more information, etc.). Your dynamic blog needs to be professional looking with good graphics but more specifically great content that changes on a regular basis. Search engine optimization needs to be part of your maintenance plan and have links to your social media. Optimize your site for mobile phones because people are shopping with their phones while they wait for the bus, sit at the airport and even sitting in their backyards. The primary focus of any social media program is to engage, engage and engage your viewer at every opportunity. Make them want to follow you, visit your blog and most importantly buy from you.

The bottom line with social media is that it's all about Social. Engagement equals likeability and customers. Your content needs to be great and remember your audience. This is the age of enlightenment for entrepreneurs – carpe diem!

Social Media Platforms by the Numbers

These numbers are current at 2017. The numbers in the brackets are stats from 2014:

- **Pinterest** – 150 Million Active Users (**+80** Million Active Users)
- **Twitter** – 313 Million Active Users (**-247** Million Active Users)
- **Facebook** – 1.86 Billion Active Users (**+860** Million Active Users)
- **YouTube** – 1 Billion Active Users
- **Instagram** – 700 Million Users (**+450** Million Active Users)
- **Google+** – 375 Million Active Users (**-25** Million Active Users)
- **LinkedIn** – 400 Million Active Users (**+227** Million Active Users)

While the numbers seem to tell a less than glorious story for Google and Twitter the statistics are more of an overall indicator. With hundreds of millions of followers it is hard to tell active users from robots and the definition of 'active' is also in question.

What is the bottom line? These are huge numbers of people who are on social media platforms.

Grab your favorite social media platform and focus your attention on that one. Don't forget the others because they all have a special way you can make them work for your company. The thing is social media has provided anyone to become an expert on a social platform of heir choosing and create change where they find it.

Back in the old days of big advertising agencies determining how we eat, sleep and purchase we had little influence unless we were celebrities. With Twitter and the rest of the social media platforms we have evolved into brand ambassadors, influencers and people who have the capacity to make change happen in our communities, our countries and the world. If we can create change in large-scale areas like our countries we can easily make change happen to the companies we like, the products we use and the brands we purchase.

What Are Brand Influencers?

Brand influencers are really "value-added influencers" such as journalists, academics, industry experts, trendsetters or those with extensive social circles. If you can find these individuals, there are no limits to your brand's reach.

As brand influencers who have built authority with a target audience and have earned trust in communities relevant to specific businesses you can yield incredible returns.

Recent research conducted by Ipsos across 23 countries globally shows that Brand Influencers tend to be more highly educated than average, with above average income. They are also more socially active and informed. They are present in all age groups, young and old, but are more likely to be men than women in most countries – but not in all.

Are You a Brand Influencer?

If you are any of the below, you could be a brand influencer.

- **Experts:** These are the authorities in a certain subject, and people look to these experts for information, advice, and guidance.
- **Activists:** influencers get involved, with their communities, political movements, charities and so on.
- **Connected:** influencers have large social networks
- Impact: influencers are looked up to and are trusted by others
- **Active minds:** influencers have multiple and diverse interests
- **Trendsetters:** influencers tend to be early adopters (or leavers) in markets
- **Conference and event speakers:** Trusted & respected by others
- **Positional Influencer:** is often in the person's inner circle. Friends, family, spouses are all examples of positional influencers.

The cool thing about all these types is that some do not require huge followers to be an influencer and some influencers also cross several of these types.

Now that you know what kind of influencer you can be, or are, you need a plan to go with it.

Chapter 3 – Planning Your Social Media

It's like any plan you'll ever make. When you devise a social marketing plan you will need to treat it like a well organized guide including goals, demographics, vision, time set asides to manage it as an integral part of another plan, your marketing plan. I am a firm believer in developing a Business Plan for any venture. Social media covers all social media from Twitter to the picture based Instagram and everything in between. Choose the platforms that work for you and ones in which you have a strong interest.

Social media is a tough thing to master for some yet others find it fascinating and fun. The issues come to the forefront when you are trying to use social media for business and you are not sure if you are doing things right, are on track or making your branding worse. Some of my colleagues are reticent to use any social media because they don't understand it but realize the power. They realize from news reports the problems you may encounter if you 'say the wrong thing' or people interpret your message incorrectly. My mantra for a years has been, "All that is not Said is Lost". I have lost thousands of followers because I gave my opinion whether it is right or wrong.

Entrepreneurs using social media for making sales or generating leads can often feel like it takes forever and it is far more time consuming than they figured. Take heart - if you set some goals, follow some simple steps and work on only the social media that directly affects your business (and you enjoy) then it won't become a daily chore for you, but an opportunity to enhance your business and engage with new friends.

Taking care of your social media will help it take care of you. Follow the points below and it will give you some valuable insights in your own social media and give you some ideas for growth. Dig as deep into this as you feel comfortable.

What Social Media Platform to Use for Your Business

I'm going to assume that you are not a big corporation with a pile of IT people who double as your Social Media gurus who plan out your entire business strategy for you.

I hear all kinds of advice on how to either brand your business or bring in more customers. Of course, branding your business well will bring in more customers but they are two different animals. Branding will tell people about you and provide name recognition but you must have an offering for people to actually buy your product or service.

When you look at social media, some are better than others to give you both results. I like using Twitter for branding because of its vast reach and immediacy. It gives my brand personality and allows me to engage directly with followers. Heaven forbid though if I start trying to sell things to my many followers. It's not fickleness that would make them stop following me; rather it's not expected from me. I try to give people good content to help them make better businesses decisions. I think Twitter is ideal as a customer service tool and business should stick to it for that while giving good information away. Twitter is about engaging people for me and I enjoy it.

Twitter is a micro-blogging social site. At 140 maximum characters the micro part is pretty obvious. But if you look at US President Trump's tweets you can see that a person can pack a big wallop (or get into trouble easily) in those few characters. The largest penetration of Twitter has always been centered in the US but it is slowly but steadily spreading. Happy Tweeters manage to fire off 6000 Tweets a second on this platform.

Twitter has five main functions: your timeline in chronological order, notifications, moments, messages and your profile. The 140 character limit may contain, text, links, videos and photos. Each user has a 'handle' as an identifier. Most people have interesting handles though I simply use my full name because I am branding myself. Other users can 'mention' you in a Tweet by placing the '@' sign in front of your name. This will then populate in your 'notifications'.

Every Tweet by other users allows you to ReTweet it, quote or 'like' the initial Tweet. Hashtags '#' are placed before a name, message, campaign to allow it to be searched by others. When you search a particular hashtag every tweet with the # will come up. If a lot of people use the same hashtag then the topic will 'trend'. During 2017's Super Bowl LI you could follow the game with the hashtags #Brady,

#Falcons, #Patriots and #SuperBowl to see all the Twitter action.

Tweet chats are topic oriented with a host who determines the time and date of a chat. This is an opportunity to do some organic advertising and is followed by any size group of like-minded people who are interested in the topic. This chat is a live event and is a great time to share your insights an opinion while promoting your own brand.

Monitoring your brand on Twitter is a tough act to manage. It's a 24 hour a day platform with massive amounts of new content every second so you need to be on top of it that's why Hootsuite, Buffer, Sproutsocial and other aggregators are good management tools. Since messages change so often it's important to catch 'mentions', thank new followers and respond to them immediately. It's a great opportunity to engage with users and share new content with them.

Twitter Lists and ads round out the platform. Lists are categorized lists you create to make finding you influencers easier. My lists include, authors I follow, entrepreneurs who stand out and media I can connect with for press releases, etc. Ads are the typical way the platforms earn money. It's relatively cheap to advertise on Twitter and the conversion rate to buy your product or follow you is high.

Using Twitter I have changed Canadian Law (Bill C470), held restaurants, hotels and car dealers accountable to customers and helped conscientious businesses provide better service to their valued and valuable customers. If I see injustice I am quick to point it out to whoever will listen however, if the companies I admonish wok with me I will tell my followers that too. It's all about being treated fairly.

Sometimes it's not a good idea to be too opinionated on Twitter, people can easily hide behind their avatar and attack people for their views. I commented on President Obama in an uneven light once and had 900 emails from furious supports of the US President.

As a company or small business you need to stay away from topics that may alienate any of your followers. Obviously religion, immigration, politics and anything sexual will mess you and you business up.

Since it is so immediate you can have a chat with anyone on twitter but fair warning it can be seen by everyone and your followers may not be too impressed by a number of tweets to a fellow tweeter about your new car or last night's hockey game.

Snapchat recently did an IPO and went public raising billions for its owners. Snapchat is a fast growing platform that some may say is the weirdest social media platform out there. The user sends videos, photos and text that disappears with in 1-10 seconds depending on what duration the user set – What? How can a platform that doesn't store content and lasts such a short time be effective as an engagement tool? Don't blink or you'll miss it! The demographics for Snapchat are 18 - 34 year olds, I guess they like the immediacy of the platform. They can send the 'snaps' to their friends or create a story over a 24-hour period. It's a challenge to market to Snapchat because it's an intense way to view content. It's growing its following by users posting their user id's to other social media platforms. The thing that I was amazed at is your snap can be taken over by high volume users who will promote your business by sending the snaps to their networks.

Google + is another brand-oriented platform, so again, don't try selling something to your followers. It is quality driven original content and people are looking for exactly that. They won't tolerate re-used content. This social network allows brands and users to build circles of influence defined as friends, family, business or following. Google+ is growing rapidly but brands have not been fast on the uptake to leap on board. The platform itself is growing very rapidly. This might be a good place to give them a freebie like that white paper you were working on. Remember this platform, being owned by Google, is a good searchable product that you can easily use and will gain you some SEO traction.

LinkedIn.com is a career and business-oriented social networking site. Whether you have a job, plan to start a business, are well established in business and want to grow your business this is the place to be. It's even a vast source for educators and universities and recruiters love it. LinkedIn although business focused is still a very social network. Brands that are participating are mainly corporate brands giving potential and current associates a place to network. The surprising fact of LinkedIn is that 79% of the users are 35 and older.

It's very much like Facebook in that it gathers like-minded individuals but it differs in that its focus is on business, career and networking. I secured a major client (a foreign government) from my profile on LinkedIn. LinkedIn is a source of fodder for Recruiters and Headhunters seeking the new CEO of that new media corporation.

LinkedIn is strongly targeted to business versus a friend-type database. LinkedIn is one of my favorites. Some consider it the ultimate resume for those looking for employment but I have found many like-minded people wanting to invest in my projects or offer advice when needed. I think quality information dissemination is key here. Don't be afraid to sell your product or service here – we all do. By the way, it is a considerable resource of job seekers with an estimated 85% of all recruiters being on LI.

LinkedIn is invitation-only based and LinkedIn tries to protect this status. Don't try following too many people you don't have any connection to as they might complain. I have 4 simple letters after my profile name - LION. This is an open invitation to people who want to do business with me to type in my email address and I will connect with them. LION means LinkedIn Open Networker. They occasionally remove it from my profile to maintain the systems integrity. I don't mind, I just put it back up there for another 6 months until they remove it again, lol.

Another good feature of LinkedIn is the ability to 'publish' a lengthy article. I often rewrite one of my blog posts and repurpose it for LinkedIn. While I get about 8000 visits a month, heaven knows what the range my article will reach on LinkedIn but I think it is in the million range. This is another good point to consider; when you write good content try to repurpose it in different ways. You can't simply copy and paste articles without changing them a bit because Google will notice it.

LinkedIn will also allow you to post interesting things like you would on Facebook. It allows you to share to the people you are connected with or to the public.

LI allows you to put recommendations from others right on your profile. It gives you 'social proof' and allows others to see that clients have endorsed you. Being supported and backed by your peers is a very powerful selling tool. You can ask people for a recommendation or it can come by organically, either way you have to approve it before it is posted on your profile.

LinkedIn allows you to show off projects you have done, inventions you have made and articles/books you have published. I've put my article I wrote for the Journal of Business because it is an academic validation of my skills. My two books are also prominently mentioned with my book cover to draw people to purchase them.

I was introduced to the Mayor of Mexico City through LinkedIn who needed a Westcoast connection to do a deal with some Chinese companies. He found me through LI and although our liaison failed to yield a lucrative deal it was interesting to meet some powerful people to add to my database (rolodex).

Obviously when you are profiled on a very powerful site and take full advantage of its' features, traffic will be sent to wherever you want, whether it's your blog post, website or a landing page with your sales pitch. It's all good. I see a dramatic spike (like 800-1000 people) of visits to my blog within 5 minutes of a post on LinkedIn.

As with all my social media platforms, I use each platform to share my content. Twitter content gets posted with some added length, FB content is there, Instagram photos and then they are all cross-collateralized for maximum effect. It's an overused term but with the right content on this profile you can become a 'thought-leader' in no time and that means money.

I have built wonderful relationships with people from LI. There's no BS because we all put our reputations on line with this online resume. You don't get very many stupid requests or questions because your followers are typically all on the same page. You get what you give and bare in mind there are world-class experts on here. I met a fellow at a conference I was giving a keynote at and we were following each other on LI. He is considered in the top 50 thought-leaders in the world on education. That is out of 350 million people on LI – wow.

This extensive network is not just one on one connects. You are part of a group. Being part of a group gives you access to 3rd party connections that you wouldn't otherwise have the option to connect with. Under the members section of each group you can look at the member list to see who else is there, what they do, and how to connect it them. This is much like a backdoor access.

One of the features of LI is you can download your entire list as a '.csv' file so, while I don't usually do it myself, you can use this database for sending them emails. My LI following, at around 10,000, is a massive database to utilize – as long as you don't spam people.

LinkedIn is supposed to be for people who already know each other but as discussed I prefer to think of it as a growing network list of new and exciting followers to share and give valuable information. Having said that you can ask one of your followers for an 'introduction' to someone they may know that you might like to meet. As long as they are friends of that person it is a very simple request.

A perfect example of how these relationships work is I had a client in manufacturing in Vancouver who needed some specific advice from someone in the same industry. Normally it's difficult to call up your competitor to ask these questions but imagine asking the owner of a manufacturing company in England for advice? People love to talk and they love to offer advice even more, so asking someone so far away is advantageous because they are not competition and will probably relish the chat with you.

Remember this is not a one-way relationship. If you get valuable information from people on LinkedIn it is expected that you provide valuable content too. Paying it forward goes far here. If you give a simple piece of advice you may end up getting work or an endorsement from that person. You never really know whom you are giving the advice to because the profile only goes so far. They may have a follower who is your next million-dollar client. I met a future business partner on LI and we made a deal at a coffee meeting a day later.

You can search people by company that is a cool option. It is a great way to try to find that perfect person to talk to at ABC company and beats trying to get past the gatekeeper on the phone.

Meetup.com. According to Wikipedia **Meetup.com** (also called **Meetup**) is an online social networking portal that facilitates offline group meetings in various localities around the world. While it is an online network it is only that way for facilitation of setting up physical networking meetings like the old days. Meetup allows members to find and join groups unified by a common interest, such as politics, books, games, movies, health, pets, careers or hobbies. This phenomenon is incredible for linking up like-minded people in any number of locales for personal or business.

I use my Meetup, Private Equity Financing, to tell people about my workshops and seminars. It's easy to schedule events with a handy calendar, booking system, email distribution to my 'followers' and allows me to charge people for the events using PayPal or provide a free workshop when I am trying to build up interest for a product or service I am offering. Information sessions are a great way to advertise your products and services and of course it's not a good idea to charge people for what should be a free meeting because you are trying to sell them something.

In my office at Kickstart we did a daily 'scrum', like a huddle in football, where anyone in the office drops what they are doing and formed a circle. We introduced ourselves; told the others what we were doing and what we needed help with for the day. It was cool because we had a permanent 11am scheduled scrum on our Meetup page. We find that if people are in the area, want to see what we are up to or want to be part of a community it was a good way to meet new people. Since the scrum Meetup is consistent people felt comfortable just dropping in. There might be anywhere from 5-15 people in the scrum and it generally lasted 30 seconds per person. All this brings me to Facebook.

Facebook is the mother of all social media. Everyone seems to be on Facebook. I have a love/hate relationship with Facebook. It's timeline bugs me and I don't like the personal info or pics people expect on Facebook - but it is the largest place for opportunities to communicate with consumers in a non-obtrusive way.

I have a low-key profile page with about 4000 followers and a business page. Truth is I use both to 'push' business info to people and I tend to use this more for selling. FB has an incredible community after all but many people are not aware of its intense ad campaign possibilities. You can 'target' people down to their neighborhood for your product or service. The cost to advertise is based on your need and budget and there is a budget for everyone. Sometimes I will buy ads based on $5/day and other campaigns I might allocate $75/day. Like I say it's affordable.

The cool thing about Facebook ads is you can use geocaching to find people that meet your demographics to reach even your neighborhood. Imagine target clients as to age, likes, marital status and location within a mile of your business?

The choices are yours how you want to run your social media but for me I play with what I like and find that mix of the triad, Twitter, LinkedIn and Facebook. They work best for my dual purpose of branding and acquiring customers.

If you are visually oriented Pinterest and Instagram are your favorite social platforms. **Pinterest** is a social site all about discovery. People pin photos into collections called boards, which serve as big catalogs of objects. Pinterest, in effect, decomposes web pages into the objects that are embedded in them. With 68% of users being female it's not wonder that the largest opportunities on Pinterest is for décor, babies, weddings, recipes and fashion. It is all about gorgeous images that you can 'pin' to your own 'pinboard'. The backend of Pinterest is really exciting because it's a collection of what people have or want, a database of intentions and a marketer's dream. With 150M users you must check it out. I 'pin' images of guitars, mainly Gibson guitars to my Pinterest account.

Instagram, as I said is like Pinterest but is four times larger and is all about pictures and 60 second videos. Most brands using this social media site use #Hashtags and post pictures that consumers can relate to with a hashtag for easier search capabilities.

Your Social Media Profiles

1. Make sure all your social media platforms are complete. Some social media actually tell you when you need to finish it like LinkedIn. Considering you often don't know who are reading your profile it's good to offer everything you feel is relevant to your brand and company. I was taking on four MBA students the other day for a practicum over the summer. At our first meeting I was amazed how much they knew about my businesses and me. They had researched me through LinkedIn. It was very flattering and impressed me to know they took the time and effort to check me out.

2. Make sure your social media is consistent, e.g. you have the same profile pic on each site and the same logo if you are using one. I met a guy at a social media event that I was presenting at and he didn't believe it I was really me, Annoyed that he would say that he pointed out an old picture on an obscure social media site that had me wearing different glassed and longer hair. Ok I got the point so although I felt he was nitpicking I guess it is correct to be consistent.

Who Does Social Media Well?

1. **Check out your top 10 influencers in your industry**, someone you like to follow and who has a good number of followers. I've met some very good people by doing this. An old acquaintance, George Moen, became friends because we had a friendly competition on Twitter and had a lot of fun engaging each other online. While this is not exactly what I meant when I said follow influencers it is safe to say that if you follow influencers in your field who have large followings the followers are more likely to follow you as well.

2. **Check their content, number of tweets and images** they use. Is this something you can emulate? There is a lot of content out there and if you can share their content and/or see what they do successfully it's better than re-inventing the wheel. Successful influencers will probably have determined over time the best times to tweet and the number of tweets and RT's that will engage their following.

3. **Ask the big guys their secrets** – we all have a couple. If I have said this once I have said it a thousand times, people love talking about themselves. If you can actually meet an influencer at a networking

event ask them for a few tips. We all give them away because it makes for a better experience for all of us if social media is done correctly and well.

Your Social Media Action Plan

Make an action plan for improvements and goals for your profiles.

1. **Locate all your social media**, can you? I'm sure you can remember the easy ones like Twitter, Facebook, LinkedIn, Google+, Instagram but what about some of the secondary sites, (hope I don't offend anyone) like Quora, Pinterest, Periscope even YouTube.

2. **Do a Google search of your name** to make sure you have them all. This may sound crazy but I forget when I sign up for those social media sites I just mentioned and find them when I do my search. I check out myself every month on Google as a way to make sure I'm not being abused or my profiles are not being hijacked – it happens! I've also found my content on other's sites, more often that not they have given me a by-line and added my photo with a short biography but once in a while I find bad guys using my stuff. I put secret digital watermarks on my material so I can find interlopers.

Keeps them on their toes.

3. I've seen people actually **put all their social media in a spreadsheet** complete with followers, dates, passwords, etc. Seems like a lot of work to me although I do have a spreadsheet for my passwords. My wife thinks I'm crazy because with all of the secure apps like Last Pass, eWallet, DataVault, mSecure, etc. there's no need to remember all the passwords you should be changing on a regular basis.

4. **Deleting some accounts** – I've enrolled in last count about 150+ social media sites. I never use some and find others a waste of time but, as I think about it, I rarely cancel my membership. It makes sense to cancel, I suppose, but I figure it's good to have my profile out there for people to see if nothing more; or is it? What if the profile is not up to date?

   Once you have deleted some sites try **refocusing** the ones you are keeping in order consolidating your brand. While being everywhere sounds exciting it is tough to manage and be great at them all.

5. Go through the **settings of the social media** you are keeping and decide if they work for you or need to be

customized. I found the link from my Facebook posts to Twitter by accident and love that feature. Are all avatars the same?

6. **Are you branded** in tune with the social media sites you're on? LinkedIn is more of a professional network for business while Twitter is casual. Again make sure your images; logos are consistent but edited for each site. I used to have a little Twitter bird perched on my shoulder on my Twitter profile pic then thought better of it since some clients expected a more business image from me.

7. How is your **social profile performing**? It is very difficult for most small business owners to keep track of highly advanced logarithms and statistics when it comes to social media return on investment (ROI). It usually comes down to measuring how much time you spend on it compared to how many sales you can actually track to it. You can track your sites and see improvements by the easiest way; number of followers and the increase over time, your engagement with others on a regular basis and frequency of your engagement. If the last two items are low maybe you should try a social media site you like and enjoy working on better. I know some friends of mine hate

Twitter and love FB – I am the opposite so I spend more time on Twitter. A program like Klout (klout.com) can help you manage those numbers.

In addition to these goals, your tune-up could also lead to more immediate action plans. You may choose to update your social background images or shift your focus to a network where more of your target market engages. Sure, the long-term measurement of these changes might not be the same as follower growth or engagement, but the improvement made to your profile is right in line with what audits are all about.

A SWOT Analysis

SWOT for the uninitiated means Strengths, Weaknesses, Opportunities and Threats. The first two are internal, meaning about you and the later two are external forces you have no control over. One of the best tools I have ever seen and one I use almost daily is the SWOT analysis. It's great for any type of problem but is very helpful in determining the best way to go forward with your social media once you have identified your audience, which platforms you like and more.

Understanding your social media and/or business from the perspective of your Strengths and Weaknesses, and the

<u>social media's</u> Opportunities and Threats (SWOT) analysis is the first step. Using a quadrant on a piece of paper you can easily brainstorm your SWOT. If you know your weakness is not being a great writer because English is your second language you will need to mitigate by hiring a good writer for your company or switching to a social media platform that writing is not as critical – like Twitter or Instagram.

Knowing that your strength is interpersonal skills would be a good fit for any social media especially if you could relate to people on YouTube face to face. If you have exceptional strengths doing a specific job work with a partner who likes the side of the business you are not comfortable doing. Sales always come to mind because it appears you must be 'born a salesman'.

The Opportunities and Threats are external forces you have no control over but you need to mitigate those in any strategic social media plan. Take for instance you are solely focused on Twitter (hands up please) and you noticed that revenues have been falling and people are talking about their flawed sales model, then heaven forbid it 'goes under'. That is a threat! What do you do if all of your media strategies are focused around Twitter?

You mitigate the problem by reducing your reliance on Twitter by being strategic with Facebook as well or an equally large platform.

Alternatively, if you are really tuned into your client's persona and know what they want and how to reach them imagine your delight when a new social media comes out of left field and you are able to not only notice it for its potential but swiftly switch to using that as a backup or more for your social media.

SWOT is a very strong tool - embrace it, it's free. Also start to embrace who you are speaking to. Your followers will have a general profile and demographic. The next thing you want to think about is which generations you are speaking to.

> *"If Plan A doesn't work,
> the alphabet has 25 more letters."*
>
>
>
> **Claire Cook**
> American Author of *Life's a Beach*

Chapter 4 – Working with the Four Generations
(Gen Z, Millennials, Gen X and Baby Boomers)

With over 2.3 billion users on social media platforms, it is definitely a challenge to market to all of them, Everyone from Gen Z to Baby Boomers like me have different preferences and need different ways to market to them

Who has the most control over people? Baby Boomers of course, <u>we</u> have the most wealth, have more time on our hands and there are a lot of us. In Canada, we have just become the largest demographic. Generation X (born 1965-1980) to a lesser degree do all the hiring, make all the decisions in business and are controlling most of the business and social controls in the world.

In 2015, social networks earned $8.3 billion (BrandWatch) from advertising. Online ad spending for social networks will exceed $35B in 2017.

Let me reiterate what age groups we're talking about here (youngest to the oldest):
- Generation Z – born between 1998 – 2004 (gee, I have socks that old)
- Millennials (also known as Gen Y) – born between 1981-1997
- Generation X - born between 1965-1980
- Baby Boomers - born between 1946–1964

What Are the Generations and How to Market to Each

Let's look at some of the characteristics of each in an effort to know how to market to them.

1. Generation Z (1998 – 2004) - It's really hard to determine anything from the youngest group worth monitoring for buying habits – the Gen Z (1998-2004). They are definitely the most connected group to technology and probably won't ever have heard of most of the technology that was replaced by disruptive technology. If your business sells products or services to this group then research like crazy because they are different from the rest. They are more likely not the main purchasers anyway, consider the parent.

2. Millennials (also known as Gen Y) (1981-1997) – These were the early adopters of Social media; they grew up with social media. You also may have noticed that they were the first generation to grow up without software manuals. Manufacturers knew from the beginning that they were intuitive learners so didn't feel the need to print costly manuals and only made digital ones available if they asked for them. Have you seen the movie about Facebook's Zuckerberg? He made Facebook for college kids.

Millennial kids are known as incredibly sophisticated, technology-wise, immune to most traditional marketing and sales pitches...as they not only grew up with it all, they've seen it all and been exposed to it all since early childhood.

Millennials are much more racially and ethnically diverse and much more segmented as an audience considering expansion in Cable TV channels, satellite radio, the Internet, e-zines, etc. came in their cycle.

They are less brand loyal and the speed of the Internet has led them to be similarly flexible and changing in its fashion, style consciousness and where and how it is communicated with.

Don't forget to optimize for mobile. More than a quarter of Millennials use mobile as their primary device for viewing content. Millennials preferred mode of connecting to the Internet is the Smartphone and tablet.

Millennials, particularly, expect information to come free. They expect free samples before buying, games and contests with prizes. Millennials like tech content 71% more than boomers. Millennials are eager to connect with Baby Boomers for business contacts. I get lots of LinkedIn invitations from Gen Millennials, including students, after networking events. Oh, and Millennials are more likely to get into trouble at work – they share everything – a blur of personal and professional.

Millennials tend to think whatever they do is news and worthy of an update to their world. Millennials use social media for invitations, checking in at venues, meeting up and getting recognition for use.

Millennials have the most Facebook friends of any generation, and 87% of Millennials (stats from Hootsuite) use the platform.

User generated Content

Like Generation Z, Millennials are also fans of User Generated Content (UGC), believing that it is 50% more trustworthy[1] and 35% more memorable than branded imagery.

If you're looking to reach Millennials on social media, consider creating a UGC campaign on Facebook or creating custom Facebook advertisements designed to reach your target audience. USG is any form of content such as blogs, wikis, discussion forums, posts, chats, tweets, podcasts, digital images, video… It's also a good idea to link to your online store and products in your social media posts since each millennial spends an average of $2,000 online each year.

3. Gen Xers (1965-1980) – They are the kids of Baby Boomers, were quoted by Newsweek as "the generation that dropped out without ever turning on the news or tuning in to the social issues around them." Gen X is often characterized by high levels of skepticism, "what's in it for me" attitudes. Gen Xers are probably the best-educated generation with 29% obtaining a bachelor's degree or higher.

Generation X uses Twitter as a primary content sharing platform 70.4 percent more than Baby Boomers. Millennials

---

[1] 50% more trustworthy: https://blog.hootsuite.com/how-to-engage-any-demographic-with-a-social-media-campaign/

X is skeptical — likes Twitter

prefer sharing memes 54.7 percent more than Baby Boomers. Generation X likes sharing slide-shares 49.6 percent more than Millennials. Gen x uses Twitter as primary sharing platform 71% more than boomers

4. Baby Boomers (1946–1964) Ok so we are old fashioned, we prefer to connect using a laptop or a desktop (remember those?) and from my observations will be older, outdated models. Baby Boomers have access to 70% of the nation's disposable income. Boomers also use Google+ as a primary content sharing platform 92 percent more than Millennials. Boomers prefer sharing images and videos the most. Boomers like world news 95% more than Millennials.

- Boomers tend to separate professional and personal information on sites. Younger generations make less distinction between professional and personal.
- Boomers are more concerned about privacy.
- They are not as continually on social media.
- They may have different notions of what's news.
- There is more "selling" from the younger generations on social media. (One of Gen Y's labels is "Generation Sell.")
- Boomers are active on LinkedIn and are business and job-oriented.
- Boomers need to become more concise in their

messaging (think 140 characters) and use more visuals.
- While Boomers don't care for Instagram, 41% of Baby Boomers have Pinterest accounts, so you might consider Pinterest marketing campaigns as well.
- This generation is also becoming more tech savvy with 54% of older Americans owning Smartphones, up from only 35% in 2011. And 84% of Baby Boomers maintain profiles on Facebook. Funny about that but I use it to see if any of old school chums are still alive!
- In addition, 58% of Baby Boomers are willing to visit a company's website after encountering the brand on social media. So if you want Baby Boomers to visit your website, just include a link in your Facebook advertisements.

From Gen Z to the Boomer generation there is a consistency across all generations for top and bottom content streams. All generations agree 300 words is the optimum size for articles. I must be odd since I love longish articles and blog posts that actually have meat on them. I also question the webinar not being as popular as I might have thought but then again I am a Boomer <sigh>.

The Top Content Forms All Generations Like:
- Blog articles
- Images
- Comments
- eBooks
- Audiobooks

The Bottom Content Forms All Generations Like:
- Quizzes
- Webinars
- Slideshares
- Webinar
- Whitepapers

Specific Content for Each Generation

This is a list of top category content leaders and who likes what:
- Entertainment - Millennials
- Technology - Millennials
- World News – Baby Boomers
- Healthy Living – Gen X
- Comedy - Millennials
- Politics - Baby Boomers
- Sports – Millennials
- Local news – Baby Boomers

[Handwritten note at top: The average attention span of a Gen "Z" is eight seconds]

- Personal Finance = Gen X
- Environment – Millennials

What Generations Like the Most

Gen Z – Like brands to reach them by email and 25% left Facebook. The average Generation Z'er has an attention span of eight seconds, so social media marketers have to quickly grab their attention with creative, interactive content. This is why visual social platforms like Instagram, Vine, and YouTube resonate with Generation Z.

To reach this generation, marketers can create user generated content campaigns and incentivize participation. This is a great way to capitalize on Generation Z's talents and encourage them to interact with your brand on social media.

- **Millennials** – Express themselves and express likes and dislikes about lifestyle. 87% use Facebook.
- **Gen X** – Get informed and go with events and trends
- **Baby Boomers** – Leisure, friends and family, videos

Communicators make a lot of mistakes when trying to reach the demographic suitable for their product or service. Some of these are:

- Not challenging assumptions about who uses social media and who doesn't and how.

- Using only one message and one format. Offer a choice of media; though video seems to be taking over, it is not everyone's preferred way of learning. I switch around formats all the time.
- Not varying the degree of directness of a "sell." Older generations especially need to develop a relationship first.
- Not considering the image of celebrities and spokespeople used so that the audience relates (young, old, thin, athletic, etc.).

Social media and its use will continue to evolve and become even more central to our lives in positive and negative ways, depending on your viewpoint. Creating situationally relevant metrics for ROI and trying to get away from checking your Smartphone 17 times a day for new messages will always be a challenge. Save your energy to adopt some good habits that we will discuss around basic engagement - don't worry I have a checklist!

Chapter 5 – A Basic Checklist for Social Media Engagement

There are 34 items on the following check list. Use this checklist for your social media engagement plan.

1. Types

I like to have lists of target 'types' of people who I want to connect to or rather engage. To connect you must understand them. If you are going to utilize Twitter, simply enter a search item in the Search Engine on Twitter and follow people who come up. I like to follow 'entrepreneurs' and we all tend to stick together so about 30- 40% of those I follow will follow me back. By targeting types of people that I would find interesting, I assume that they will follow me back if we have the same interests. Having said that, this is not about creating lists. It's about finding people that spur your interest, give you interesting feedback and/or discussions and are engaging with other like-minded people. My lists include entrepreneurs, authors, writers and hi-tech business owners, all subjects I regularly tweet or chat about on my blog.

My search words for my Twitter following are pretty simple. I use words like startup, financing, investing, entrepreneurship and others related to these.

2. Engagement

Engage people about important things to you every day in a two-way conversation on Twitter for 10 minutes. Engagement may seem like a buzzword but it's a true measure of a social media type to engage in conversation with someone in a meaningful way. It's not good enough to just say "hi how are you doing". I often click on the person's Twitter name that takes me to their profile instantly. Once there I feel a little more connected to them often because the 'handle' they use on twitter may not have their name but the profile does. When I send @rainmaster a Tweet to engage but call her by her name it impresses her because she knows I have gone to the trouble to find out more about her. I now am on the way to having a relationship with this person. I find it amusing when I go to a networking event wearing my own personalized nametag with only my twitter name and a very large QR code. People with whom I may have 'engaged on Twitter come up to me and introduce themselves. It's kind of fun to be able to put a name to a face. I've met some wonderful people that way. For heaven's sake don't sit there like a lump reading tweets all day without engaging yourself. People who sit idly by afraid to comment are called 'trolls' by those of us who care. I realize it is scary out there in the real world and often if you make a comment on Tweeter there will be people who may call you out on it but hey, it's like giving someone the finger when you are driving – it doesn't matter until you stop side by side at a traffic light.

3. Profiles and Networks

Remember when we used to network in person? Join a social media site once a week and develop it completely meaning put your real name and contact information, tell people what you like and what bothers you in the world – put your self out there. I must belong to about 100 social media sites. I may not be active in that many of them but each one of them has a complete profile of me on them. There's nothing worse than seeing a profile minus a face picture or missing a profile. One problem with the idea of joining lots is that you need to keep in touch with your profiles so that when things change in your life, albeit a new job or position you can quickly keep people up to date with your life changes. It backfires too. Recently, I made a change on my LinkedIn account and over the next three days I received well over 300 'congrats' emails from followers. Although the sentiment is wonderful and much appreciated I felt compelled to respond to all 300 if only to say thanks for thinking of me. That's a lot of time expended.

4. Tracking Stats

Join websites that monitor and track your statistics to know where you are in relation to others Klout, Dashboard on Blog, etc. Twitter allows you to find out about your analytics just by going to your settings on your Twitter account. You can easily see what your best Tweet was, the reach your account is getting, when was the best time to Tweet, etc. Klout is a cool website/tool that gives you stats on people following you on Twitter, the amount of 'real' people you influence and other great stats. Rated from 1-100 depending on your influence with people (meaning do they follow your advice, do they ReTweet your posts, etc.) you can be assured that someone with a rating of over 70 is someone who has consistently given out good information and has a steady following. At this writing mine is 70. Check it out at http://klout.com. I use the 'dashboard on my blog to keep abreast of comments on my

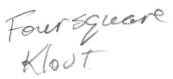

blog, stats on who is visiting, what part of my blog they are visiting etc. If you're not getting visitors - why not? I often send a post on Twitter about a topic I've written on my blog. I call it 'pull' marketing because I'm trying to draw people or pull them to my website. Push marketing on the other hand is when I send them an offer of a book or video for a price.

5. Use Google Alerts to Monitor

Unless you really want to mess up or have only 10 followers on your social media site, monitor what is being said about you and your business on Google Alerts. I am on a social media site called Foursquare which allows you to check into places, become mayor by having a number of visits, get specials, e.g. restaurant discounts and you can leave comments. I showed a friend and GM of a very large Vancouver Restaurant, this website and some of the comments that had been made. Firstly, I was surprised he had not heard of the iPhone app and secondly he was very surprised when I showed him that I was the Mayor of his restaurant and that there were 10 comments about the food and staff. Wow, what an awakening he had when he looked at the bad comments about a certain dish. No one had complained about the food or service, rather they posted them on a social media site for the world to see. You need to keep an eye on things that can affect you personally.

6. Check your eMail

I **MUST** check my email several times a day on my Smartphone or I will go into convulsions! Answer Email ASAP. I have a client who had a message on his phone saying if he didn't answer the phone he was busy and that he only responds to messages at 1pm and 6pm. He had the same message on his email. The result was people didn't want to do business with him because he was not accessible enough in this instant gratification society we now live in.

If you're in business damn well answer your phone and mail immediately. The rule of thumb I tell my clients is to answer all emails whether it is just an acknowledgment within 2 hours. Some large corporations in Vancouver told me that the rule of thumb is to respond to all email within 72 hours. Those policies give me the willies because I will go somewhere else.

7. Professional Photo

Pay for one professional photo for all of your Social media and keep it current. This is a no brainer. I asked a friend how to increase my Twitter followers, he told me to drop the suit and tie pic I had in my profile because no one will follow a business guy all suited up. I took his advice and have at this writing 500,000 Twitter followers. A professional portrait is inexpensive when you consider all the places you can use it. Heck if you can't afford a really good one go to the Sears Portrait Studio and use the free one they give you. Mine cost me $90 with 3 different poses.

8. Set up a Website/Blogsite

If you aren't tech savvy hire someone to develop a professional looking Blog for you. **WordPress** is very easy to get the hang of for people with limited abilities. I laugh at the prices people pay for websites and blogs today. I used to charge $50,000 for an average website now the same one can be had for $1000. Blog templates can be purchased for under $100 and are so easy to use because they were designed for the average guy to use it on a daily basis. I use WordPress because it is a dynamic website that is constantly changing because of your blog writing. Did I say blog writing? See number 5.

9. Write Blog Posts Weekly

Write one blog post once or twice per week on a relevant topic, of course this is a guide, often I don't blog for 3 weeks but blog on 3 topics, this keeps the site fresh and keeps

Content is Key!

bringing people back that is your goal. Blogs took websites to the next level, interaction and immediacy. If you write interesting pieces on your blog and I'm not talking about what you had for lunch (unless you run a foodie blog) people will come back another day to see what else you have written. People don't care if your writing is poor as long as you give them content – Content is King! By changing your blog every week you make it dynamic rather than a website that sits there and does nothing, once its seen people go, blogs bring people and customers back.

10. Provide A Free Offer in Return for an Email

Provide a free offering on your Blog to help you develop a database, use 'aWeber' service to 'capture' these folks' email addresses and respond to them professionally. Well, duh, you're reading my free offering, if you like it you may come back as a guest or a customer. (I hope). Since you have responded to a social media article maybe I can convince you to spend money next time on another product of mine. The good thing is you have 'opted-in' to possibly receive more offerings from me by subscribing to my list. I promise I won't offer you garbage.

11. Write Comments

If you engage other bloggers and write comments you will generate links, try commenting on 4 per week. I love responding to other people's blogs. I always get a kick out of people putting comments about a blog post – It tells me people are reading it. You should respond to the comment even just to say thanks, but engagement (there's that word again) is always welcome and really good if you something to contribute.

12. Be Nice

Be generous to other bloggers and tweeters by RT or comments. Good karma is always the best; if you don't have something nice to say don't write it, it's all about people's opinions and some can create tremendous issues. I commented on Obama on a Tweet and received 800 tweets about it and lost a 1000 followers in 5 minutes.

Alternatively if people start taking bites out of you on social media I have a great solution for you – treat them with kindness! I get people all the time coming after me, most are anonymous but the worst thing you can do is to engage with them on the same level. I have found that if you apologize or explain your opinion they will apologize to you. This is, in part, because they don't often expect you to respond and when you do especially if you have a lot of followers they are embarrassed. Others see your behavior and respect you for it.

13. Make Online Friends

This is about engagement and relationships, personally email a Reader. I have met hundreds of people online, many are now friends. I've secured contracts and sold stuff to them too. It all started with a comment, a tweet or a post.

14. Don't Ignore Twitter

Check Twitter often. Again the immediacy of Twitter is awesome. A tweet was the first news about the death of Michael Jackson; Obama claims he owed a lot to Twitter for getting elected US President and what can we say about President Trump? He certainly uses it a lot.

When I check my Tweets and traffic I always interact with someone. Since I am there anyway and check it often it makes people realize I am a real person and not a robot.

15. Send Relevant Tweets, Often

Send out around 10 tweets per day on interesting relevant topics. I rarely send out stupid tweets, like how's the weather in LA, who cares. I refer people to other businesses I know and love, I send people interesting quotes and always send loads of info on business and entrepreneurs, my particular Favorite topic.

16. Use Higher Traffic Days and Hours

Some days are higher traffic days than others. Send out more tweets 15-20 on Tuesday, Thursday and Friday. I was amazed at this. Then one of my social media stars told me college students are more often online those days and around 4 - 6 pm. Stats can tell you when to post info to get to the people you want to target. If I want to reach people in the UK, I post early morning Vancouver time, I also know China is 13 hours ahead. I actually can post the same material at four times per day at 7am, 11am, 3pm and 7pm. It reaches all the time zones that way.

17. Retweet your Blogger Follower's Posts

ReTweet at least 5 Posts from other Blogs be generous to others and it will come back to you. Being generous is very important. If you say something nice about someone they will befriend you and tell 4 others about you. That's guerrilla marketing for sure.

18. How to Surpass Twitter Limits

The limit for Twitter followers is 2000! This is an actual limit up to which gathering Followers is difficult. After 2000 is reached you can 'Follow' up to 10% of your existing Followers per 24-hour time frame. Remember this is important. Twitter feels that is must be inconceivable that anyone can know more than 2000 people (I have 8000 just in my iPhone database).

The 2000 number seems to be a hard number to get past. If you hit 2000 people that you follow it is almost impossible to gain more followers until you **reduce** your follow list. The secret to grabbing large numbers is to 'Follow' a great deal of people in as short a time as possible to mitigate your downtime (the 24 hour rule). If you were to have 40,000 followers you can theoretically follow about 400 new followers a day but it will take you a considerable amount of time to do it.

Each day 'Follow' 100 people who are interesting or relevant to you, share your goals or are in your industry. I love entrepreneurs, I managed 120 startup businesses a year at one time and all my friends are entrepreneurs. I also love business that's why so many people follow my business tweets. Keep it relevant and interesting and good people will enjoy following you and will tell others.

Program to follow Twitter followers such as Crowdfire.

There are programs to help you follow people on Twitter like CrowdFire and programs to help you manage them Hootsuite.

19. Unfollowing is as Important as Following

Once a week 'UnFollow' 100 people, who don't follow you on Twitter, you may not fit their demographic or interest level. I often go through my 'followers' and pull out people who obviously I have nothing to share with, e.g. porn stars, huge corporations, religious zealots. It's my opinion and I want to reach the right people. If you are in a growth stage it is better to follow and unfollow a much larger number. I unfollow about 7000 a week.

20. The Follow Balance

Don't follow more than follow you on Twitter. There are lots of reasons for this one of which is Twitter will think you are spamming people or are a machine. You're statistics will be drastically improved if you keep a reasonable ratio of followers and those you follow.

21. Check Facebook Daily

I like to check Facebook daily. Have new posts sent to your primary email address. I really use Facebook for 2 things, to

Facebook is for connections, not for business

have fun connecting with friends and to promote others businesses. I don't consider it really a business tool but it sure does allow me to connect with friends instead of calling them or sending emails. It keeps you engaged so you don't lose friends.

I do find Facebook is great for ads. Their marketing algorithm is far superior to anything else I've seen and you can target very accurately your customers. The geo-targeting, i.e. using a hyper-local search to find customers around your business area is very valuable.

22. Acknowledge Birthdays

Why should you acknowledge friends birthdays on Facebook? It's announced every day on your page by Facebook. I can tick a box and someone gets a nice happy birthday wish from me, how pathetic if we can't take 5 seconds to acknowledge someone on a special day. Engage, engage and engage again.

23. Join Groups and Fan Pages

Be adventurous, join groups and fan pages on Facebook, Groups on LinkedIn. I must admit joining tons of groups

Linked On Open Networker "LION"

dilutes the time I can spend on more important things but sometimes the groups are cool and interesting and I get notifications each time someone writes a comment on them, often these comments are useful in my business. It also allows me an opportunity to resend info to others it may benefit. I find that I tend to ignore my company Facebook page which makes me wonder if I shouldn't just delete the account. I think it looks bad when social media accounts show no activity for a long period of time.

24. Link In

Are you on LinkedIn? You should be. Check LinkedIn every 2 days for new email, people wanting to join. I get a notice every time someone wants to join my LinkedIn page. I am a LION, a Linked In Open Networker. This means I will accept all who want to be in my network because I feel networking is really important and by having a large following I can meet exceptional people. I met and worked with the Mayor of Mexico City because of a LinkedIn contact and query by him about my Pacific Rim connections.

I often post a Tweet or a FB comment on my LinkedIn account as an update. When I write a really good post of my blog or an article from one of the online magazines I write for I publish them as 'articles' with a 'Reprinted from ___' under the title.

25. Requests to Follow?

Accept LinkedIn requests to follow you if they make sense to you. You may not be the social butterfly I am so accept contact requests if they have some relevance to your job or business. 80% of North American Recruiters are on LinkedIn and go there first to source new 'hires'. You can actually search for company personnel on LI that is a good tool if you are considering looking for a job there or doing cold call sales to the company.

26. Business Cards to LinkedIn

Add the emails of people you have met through networking from any business card you collect into LinkedIn once a week. It's part of your database. I meet a lot of interesting business people in my Meetups and other places, why not include them in your database, they have given you their card so they must be interested in hearing from you indeed they have opted-in. If I have their card they are fair game to be invited to join my LinkedIn family.

27. Offer Answers

Go to LinkedIn's Q&A section and offer answers to questions. One of the ways to increase your profile is to be an expert. Answering questions posed by other business people if its your area of expertise will elevate you in the minds of others and draw more people to your website and profile assuming you have an offer on your website.

28. Read Posts on Your Expertise

Read other posts on LinkedIn groups in your area of expertise to remain current. This goes almost without saying but it is possible that you will find opportunity in those groups.

29. iTunes or Google Play for Apps

Go to your iTunes store or whatever you use to source new Apps weekly for your Smartphone. I love my iPhone and the app store. I have about a 100 on my phone and iPad. I have fun stuff but all of the apps are geared to extending my social media reach. I have social media aggregation software, apps to increase my productivity and apps to help me connect with others easier.

Develop a QR code for your business

30. Get a QR code

Develop a QR code for your Business Card, don't know what that is? Check it out. It's like a bar code that has an incredible amount of information on including access to your website, all of your contact information and an abundant of things important for you to get out to your customers, friends or people you meet at a tradeshow. I have a QR code printed on the back of my business card. A person I meet can quickly scan the code on a Smartphone and be taken directly to my website. An incredible feat if we are standing together at a tradeshow. By the way it's free. I'm not sure how relevant it still is but I find it an easy way to load a lot of information to an already crowded business card.

31. Start a Meetup

Start your Own Meetup for around $85/year and send out invites to join. If you are an entrepreneur in Vancouver near my office you can attend about 45 networking meetings called Meetups spread throughout the week. You can search geographically and a lot of Meetups gather for lunch, maybe in your area. You can setup your own group or join an existing one in your area of interest. I have a realtor client who joined a realtor Meetup. He likes to chat about real estate and finds it helpful, if he was hoping to get a listing or

Start a meet up

sell a house he may have opted to go to an entrepreneur Meetup or a builders Meetup. Check out http://meetup.com.

Meetup are special interest groups. While I have three company Meetups they must be educational in nature not a business vehicle per se. Companies can get around this by being the sponsor whether it is providing expertise, the venue or perhaps appetizers. It's another case of good branding. Meetup gives you an example of a Meetup description like this *"This is a group for anyone interested in hiking, rock climbing, camping, kayaking, bouldering, etc. All skill levels are welcome. I started this group to meet other outdoor enthusiasts. Looking forward to exploring the outdoors with everybody."*

I like their philosophy of what it means to be a Meetup:
- Real, in-person conversations
- Open and honest intentions
- Always safe and respectful
- Put your members first

32. SEO

Make sure your Blog/Website is Search Engine Optimized (SEO). I just talked to a new client who only ranks on Google when you type in his complete website address, nothing else. Putting good money into a blog or website then not promoting

Search Motor optimization is worth it.

it even from the most basic standpoint seems useless to me, again you don't need to spend a lot of money look around for a good SEO person and watch your traffic improve. SEO has changed over the past couple of decades so if your website is older consider getting the SEO overhauled.

33. Don't Drink and Tweet

Chardonnay Effect- OK folks so here is the clincher. I love Chardonnay wine, that invigorating beverage at the end of a tough day at the office. How many times have you wished you had not sent an email to someone or posted a tweet to someone then realized you must look like an idiot or it might come across different than you intended? OK, now add 2 or 3 glasses of wine to your judgment and see what happens, your engagement will turn into a nightmare trust me- been there and done that!

Send it tomorrow when clearer heads prevail. The most important thing about social media for me is to devote as much time as you can or feel comfortable doing and have fun.

34. Protect Your Passwords

I've been told I am a very clever guy and even an expert in social media. This item is one of my biggest lessons for you -

PROTECT YOUR PASSWORDS AT ALL COSTS and change them often. When you type a new password into your account and the little password guru tells you it's 'strong' then add something else to it to make it impregnable.

December 25, of 2011 after a night of celebrations and a little tired I logged into my Twitter account and was hit by a notice asking me if I wanted to be 'Verified' as a Twitter user. Being 'Verified by Twitter is like being validated by Twitter for being well known, possessing huge numbers or being a celebrity. In my tiredness I immediately said yes and signed into an official looking form asking me for my User Id and Password. I gave those two as requested, after all it was Twitter asking, and within one measly minute lost 160,000 Twitter followers. The form was fake, the verification bogus, in fact, it was a 'phishing' trip designed to appeal to my ego and give up my account.

The perpetrator was a 14-year-old sociopath from Los Angeles. It wasn't hard to figure out who he was even though he changed the name of my account and set up a new one for me with no followers in it. Twitter refused to do anything because the first thing he had done after changing the password was to change the email address associated with the account. Twitter identifies the account to the email address. Out of luck! I felt like crap for about 2 months, went to a lawyer, the FBI and the CIA – believe it or not I did. They all had empathy for me and my situation but Twitter held all the cards along with my 14-year-old perp. If you don't think there is a value associated to a Twitter account think again. One Tweet can cost over $300 US to a corporation looking for a brand influencer and I have sold Twitter accounts for $1.65 per follower – you do the math on a half million-user account.

I picked up myself 3 months later and embarked on a new social media campaign. At this writing I have around 500,000+ on my next iteration.

FULL SPEED AHEAD!

Chapter 6 – A Lot More About Twitter

People constantly ask me for advice on Twitter and the invariable questions about how I got to have so many followers. It is about numbers, followers and tweets and sometimes it feels like a game to get more and more followers. The thing you need to realize is that these little 140 character profiles and tweets represent real people. When I connect with someone on Twitter and they respond or give me a kind word I 'engage' them. I love that word – engage! It means a lot to me when someone thanks me for an article I have posted from some obscure source or helped a business with a bit of advice or promoted a business launch a new product.

I do put a lot of time into it but it is relative. I spend about 90 minutes a day on it in total but I reach lots of cool people from everywhere, gain incredible insight and have great conversations.

You need to have a dynamite Twitter profile. This will be what your Followers will see and from it they will decide whether to follow you or not. I had a pic of me in a suit in the beginning but while I like that image of the successful businessman I like the casual pic, it makes me feel like I am more approachable. I added a goofy little twitter 'bird' on my shoulder after some success on using Twitter and felt it was important to acknowledge Twitter. People always comment on it and remember me. Like everything though it needed to be updated so I put the bird in its cage.

Make sure your profile looks professional and has all the relevant stuff related to your business on it. I put all my information on a large graphic that is the background for my profile since the Twitter profile is so short.

I go onto Twitter when I wake up in the morning, read my overnight messages, DM's (Direct Messages) and Mentions (people who referred to me in a Tweet). Of course, I can't read them all but I quickly scan as many as I can to see if there are any really interesting Tweets or someone has asked me a question about a Tweet.

You might consider going into your Settings page when you start getting a sizable number of followers and either cancel your 'notifications' of people Following you or go into Outlook and create a Rule to move messages into a folder. I added a personal thank you with a little bit about what they can expect from me as far as content goes. This link is in 'Settings' that goes out to people who have followed you. It's meant to be an acknowledgement not a sales pitch which unfortunately most use it for.

While I am scanning my overnight Followers for interesting content I also scan for the Tweeter's locale. I want to be global but prefer to have a Canada-US centric following. When I do my work in the morning I'm cognizant of who are at work, coming home from work, sleeping, etc. If I am working on Twitter at night I'll target England that is 8 hours ahead of Vancouver. Similarly, I'd prefer to target India at a different time since they are in bed when we are just going to the office.

I then do a Search in the box provided on a topic that interests me, and usually one that is in keeping with my profile. I precede the search query with # (e.g. #entrepreneur, #startup, #business). The results show hundreds of people with the #entrepreneur in their Tweet. This is a hash tag.

I don't follow people who don't have a picture, are far removed from my business interests or show disrespect or controversy in their tweets. I stay away from large companies because they are not likely to follow me back and prefer to search and follow people who identify themselves as entrepreneurs or startups and of course business.

When you find someone quite interesting based on their profile or tweet content, it is wise to start following their followers. After all if you think they are interesting and they have a large following you can't go wrong. These followers are likely to follow you back. My buddy George Moen, a local Vancouver entrepreneur, and I have known each other for years. We had similar size followings and I'd often just follow people who followed him and I know he did the same with me because we both had similar interests and had to following the same type.

If you find the right mix of people and follow them this way you will gain large numbers relatively quickly, roughly 1500 average a week is an exceptional number with 500 doable.

This, unfortunately, causes you another dilemma; a large amount of followers with thousands more that *you* follow. Twitter likes its members to have a balance of Followers to those you Follow. You will need to find a suitable time when the internet is 'sleeping' where you must do a little maintenance – removing those who DON'T Follow you. Many times these non-followers are inappropriate Followers, robots or super niche specialty Tweeters who wouldn't follow anyone anyway.

I often do this on a Sunday night around 11 or so. Since my main focus is on North Americans most people are sleeping when I'm on the web in Vancouver at midnight. Removing Non Followers is frowned upon by Twitter but otherwise you will be stuck on 2000 Followers and 10,000 people you follow which would continue to rise at a disparate rate 3 or 4 to 1 of Following versus Followers.

You will need to download a program to **UnFollow people**. I tried one in the beginning that would delete those unfollowing folks until you stopped it with a vengeance at the rate of dozens per second. The problem was it wouldn't stop UnFollowing when you wanted it to stop. I had to turn off the computer the first time I used it so it would stop.

Twitter put a stop to this type of software in mid 2010. People were quick to stop using software they had in case Twitter decided to terminate the account of both parties, the developer of the software and the user.

You can easily find a script that will allow you to spend an hour or so to delete those who don't Follow one page at a time. Be prepared to spend time deleting these folks but guess what; as soon as you are done deleting non-Followers you can start Following people all over again. There is no limit on the number of people you can UnFollow per day. It comes down to how much time you want to spend. Google 'UnFollow' Scripts.

Recently, I have found CrowdFire, a cool social media management tool that handles Twitter and Instagram. Essentially it allows you to target specific users and follow their followers. Twitter allows you to follow 1000 people per day and unfollow as many as you want. The 1000 is a good number because based on your conversion rate you can have between 23- 64% of people you follow – follow you back. My conversion rate is roughly 64% I think because of good content and high visibility. I used to get about 3500 new followers a week, after my followers hit 450,000 it's tapered off – those darn algorithyms. You should keep a few thousand of non-followers in your account (I keep 10,000) because as you delete people to follow more there is a good chance that some of the people in that list may just not be as active as you and take a while to get around to following you. Never miss an opportunity or dismiss anyone unless you have to.

Be very careful if you use software or a service to follow people. Twitter states in their rules that any use of third party software to follow or unfollow people will result in the cancelation of your account. They used to be very tough with users and actually canceled my account once for 'aggressively' following people. It took me a week and a lot of groveling to get it back. These days Twitter must have mellowed in its 11 years because now they just stop your service and force you to change your password. They actually warn you that some may be hacking your account as a reason for doing this. It sounds so much more civilized!

Your Twitter Content

I've found that people like several things on Twitter. They like sarcasm, news with a twist, quality quotes that are witty or meaningful, good links to content rich blogs and websites and they like dialogue. After all, Twitter is immediate and relevant.

Gone are the Tweens (aren't they kids from 10-12)telling us about the kind of sandwich they are eating at school? It's been replaced by people over 35 looking for information, content, news and opportunity. Don't forget it was a Tweet that told the world of Michael Jackson's death in 2009.

After analyzing my Twitter account I know that 80% of my following are entrepreneurs (I know because I targeted them), the age demographic is between 32-52 predominantly male (64%) with an average income of about $150,000/year. This is good information to have when I want to monetize my social media as a brand influencer.

I love Quotes, but again, I try to be relevant to my topics so I might Tweet quotes about Business and then brand myself so people know it's from me, e.g. #BizQuote- "It's Not Personal, It's Business!" – Donald Trump.

The trick to viral followers is that if people like what you say they will RT (or ReTweet) your comments to all of their people. I figure I can reach more than 20 million people with one really fantastically placed RT and the right people seeing it.

You may see #FF. This means Follow Friday and is used to thank or mention to the masses other followers of you or those you admire. Of course, it is dispatched on Friday. On a recent Friday, I was ranked 13 in Canada for the number of people whom RT'ed my Tweets.

I'm constantly branding myself so I created a following for, and from, me on Tuesdays. I always felt Tuesday was much unappreciated so I fixed that oversight. Look for #BizTuesday (Biz of course is now associated to me as it is my nickname and part of my last name Bizzo). It also works well for Business so people follow me and use my #BizTuesday to mention their own friends on Tuesdays.

I like to promote businesses I like, or work with, so often I will call it "BizPik- a great massage therapist I know at

[handwritten note at top: Tweet Deck for shortening/managing tweets]

www.massagegal.com" This brings up another point. As you're aware, Tweets can only be 140 characters so I used to use TweetDeck or Hootsuite to post my Tweets. One of the features is that it takes the long URL on internet sites and reduces them to a short code to give me more space to write. Both Social media aggregators as they are called also manages other Social media like Facebook for me and keeps my Mentions; RT's and Tweets in separate columns in one interface.

Sick of Twitter?

Phew! Are you pooped or sick of Followers, Following and tweeting yet? You should be because it can be time consuming. I call it my hobby but then I have a long-term goal and my wife is very supportive so I guess you can call it my avocation.

Your Goals

So let's say you've reached 50,000 followers with some luck and a lot of hard work- now what? First thing I decided was that I was going to make a pile of money. I joined ClickBank, an affiliate marketing aggregator and sent messages out to my loyal followers trying to flog things from *increasing your Followers by 100 people a week*, (go figure) to *ebooks* on *How to Kill SilverFish*. It was an experiment for me; I tried

Click Bank for earning cash

hard and gave it a month. I made $80 in the month, alienated many of my Followers and really didn't feel good about selling snake oil.

The bottom line is when I asked for my money from ClickBank they told me I hadn't reached my payment threshold. I needed to make $100 bucks before I would be mailed a check the following month. **Take a hike guys**!

I've always believed in Engagement Marketing that is the realm of Social media. I prefer now to build my blog traffic and my reputation by 'pulling' people to me and my blog rather than using the affiliate ClickBank model of 'push' marketing product. I want people to read my stuff and buy my stuff so this model works for me.

So apparently, at this printing, I am a major influencer of others (those who follow me). I rank in the top 3 of Vancouver's 'influencers' and first in Vancouver on one list of quality Tweeters based on content. Influence is the closer of sales. Engagement Marketing which is all about influence showed that in 2003- 22% trusted "people like me" and in 2014 -87% of people trusted peer recommendations. That means if I suggest you buy something you probably will.

Oh and by the way I have made great money from Twitter,

but not in the way you think. I consulted and took over a Vancouver College a couple years ago that needed me to turn around their college and who found me on Twitter. I'd say Twitter works!

Recently, a few big companies to promote their services scouted me. PayPal approached me and offered me $250 US per Tweet for a small campaign they wanted to start for one of their new business services. I thought I had died and gone to heaven. Although the campaign worked for both of us I realized there was a problem selling myself – I had to place a statement on the bottom saying it was an ad.

#Fazioli next approached me to do a Twitter campaign with cross promotion on FB and Instagram. I thought I should approach this campaign differently. Fazioli is the world's largest and best piano company with their grand pianos selling at an average of $300,000. I envisioned and developed a campaign where me as a regular person saw one these fantastic pianos in a store window and went inside to check it out. This allowed me to get pictures for my campaign from outside looking in, sitting at the piano (thanks to the manager for the pic), me enrolling in piano classes, etc. You get the picture. Since it was a story I didn't have to make a disclaimer.

The side effect to this was that while I fell in love with the piano and became somewhat of an expert on it (it has 4 pedals and the one I played was in the movie "Fifty Shades of Grey") I engaged people on Twitter who wanted to know more about the piano, the sound, where to get one, etc. and started a real conversation. I engaged a piano teacher in Alabama and a concert pianist in Zurich. They all RT'd my observations, links and tweets and made my campaign not only viral but gave it a genuineness. While I posted several dozen tweets over the course of my 3-week campaign no one asked it they were advertising.

One of the funny side benefits of having large numbers of Followers is that often I will be mobbed at Trade shows or media conventions if I wear a badge with just my Twitter moniker - **garybizzo**. It kind of makes one feel like a rock Star; for what, a somewhat manipulated way to control and gather people who find me a little interesting. Wow!

Go forth and Tweet your face off for whatever reason you feel comfortable with. To put it in perspective Lady Gaga at this time, in 2017, has 65 million Followers, she was a Twitter nobody in 2008. There is a lot to be said for those of us who value content over fluff and treat followers like friends rather than a number.

Chapter 7 – Creating & Adding Value

As I see it there are around eight ways to create value for people that follow you on Social Media. The people with the largest followings have a mixture of several of these and mix it up regularly to make people come back for more. Remember the most important things about social media are compelling content and engagement. If you give your followers interesting and informative material they will stay with you.

The following are my rock star techniques of upping your content and engagement.

Telling a Story

I realize it's difficult to tell a story on Twitter but you can easily tell a story on your blog posts or Facebook. The thing about stories and business is that they go together to create a personal experience for the customer or follower. Share a great story of your business going out of its way for customer service or some new exciting products you started carrying, anything to engage people and giving them more reason to trust you.

I just had a carwash before settling in to write today and the attendant at the automated wash asked me if he could put some tape on a small tear in my convertible roof – duh – for sure and thank you. Then he pulled out a wrench and took off my car antennae so it 'wouldn't get bent' during the wash. I didn't even know the darn thing came off. He was at the finish of the carwash to put the antenna back on. I'm going to write about this on my blog and tell the owner of the company he works for as well. It will make a good story for the owner to post on his social media.

Having said that it's tough to tell a story on Twitter, I did create a lengthy story for my Fazioli Piano campaign that engaged people to the point that they wanted to know what was coming next. So if your story is compelling and consistent people will keep an eye out for your Tweets.

Share Your Expertise

Giving people information about what you do or the field you work in is a great way to provide followers with useful information and it raises your profile in their minds. In the olden days I used to write a short column on business for a local newspaper. I don't think I got paid for it but I was allowed to place my name and business name at the bottom of the column with the idea that if people liked the advice or information I was giving them that they might call me for more work. Writing the column raised my profile just as surely as my first book on business raised it even higher. It's no different today except that when I post content on Facebook like I did for that old column I can guarantee that more people will read it.

It's more like a passive sell whereby people will read your post and down the road will remember what you said about it and will come back to you. My buddy used to write posts about cars and how to fix certain basic problems with them that anyone could relate to. It was a popular blog and you can be sure he got customers for his auto mechanic shop from it because people knew he was an expert and could be trusted.

Answer Questions

I like this one because it happened to me the other day. I bought a relatively cheap Fender guitar for my collection and it had two real signed autographs on the guitar. I took pictures of the signatures and posted them on Twitter asking anyone if they knew whom the autographs belonged to. Within minutes I had the answer, one autograph was Stevie Vai and the other was his band-mate Eddie Van Halen. Wow, the guy that gave me the answers was my hero and I followed him and now we regularly 'engage'.

I regularly answer questions on Twitter if I can offer an answer and know that people appreciate me for taking the time. It's funny because of the high numbers of followers I have many people think I am a robot so answering question puts a real person into the equation.

Discussions

There's an art to creating discussion on social media especially Twitter. If the topic is germane to the rest of your followers it might work but lengthy discussions should probably be used on Facebook as comments. On Twitter people get perturbed following a conversation between two people for any length of time. To avoid alienating followers on Twitter switch to 'message' mode and chat away It's easier to 'get away' with extended messages on Facebook.

Sharing Tips or Hints

People love getting tips on how to do things better. Simple tips work well on Twitter and 'how to' things of course are more suited to your blog. 'How to' content never goes out of style and is considered by those in the know as 'evergreen' content. YouTube was built on 'explainer' or how to videos. This type of content draws people like flies to your social media and is considered content-rich because you can use it over and over again.

One of my posts on my blog has been read by thousands of people because it was a case study of one of my Twitter campaigns. Most of my blog posts are of the '6 ways to...' variety meaning I give people tips on how to do something be it in marketing, operations or finance. Every blog post I write is one more addition to my brand and I think is, really, the backbone of why people follow me – I'm an expert!

Make your posts your own story. Everyone has something they excel at and others are always looking for more content to feed their passion too. Consider all of the social media and how you can tap into this resource. I used YouTube to get a video out there for a client about the process of creating limited edition limited prints. People were under the impression that these prints were like mass produced posters when in fact some of the original prints were worth in the ten's of thousands of dollars. People love being educated.

Behind the Scenes

I am amazed and amused that a certain show on television about the simplest things is so popular. It's called 'How Things are Made' and it shows how everything from paperclips to electric cars are made in a simple to understand half hour format. I have been glued to that show whenever I chance upon it because they make the simplest process interesting simply because people are curious to know.

Do a short video on how your company works or a 'day in the life' of your business and get it out there. I used to be a commercial photographer and people always asked me questions about lighting, composition and camera angles, etc. so I did a few mini videos showing my setups on certain shoots. This was great because amateurs could replicate my setup themselves. Of course, they always remembered the source of their knowledge and how my little video made them look like pros.

If you look at the Kardashian phenomena and other reality shows you will understand that people want to see behind the scenes and as mundane as our daily lives seems to us others want to know. Think of the Internet as a school of voracious piranhas seeking information and I think you will understand the comparison.

Sharing Deals with Customers (or potentials)

Whenever I see a great deal online I share it with my followers. People trust me, and they figure if I like it or use it maybe it will be good for them too. Of course, the bottom line here is that unless you are sincere about the offer or use the product or service don't pretend that you do. I've had friends promote a service without knowing much about it, or even using it, and people have asked him about it at a networking meeting. He looked foolish when he couldn't answer a simple question about the product's usage.

Pay It Forward

A young man wearing a Red Cross vest and carrying the appropriate ID stopped me the other day on a busy downtown street. I knew a sales pitch was coming but I listened intently anyway. When he asked me for a measly $40 a month to 'change the world' I laughed and told him I do enough charity work. However, I did make him an offer! I told him to get his manager to give me a call and I would promote the Red Cross operation to my social media. He seemed grateful and even shook my hand but I have yet to hear from the manager.

It seems to me that paying your good fortune, or knowledge, forward is not only good for the world but will come back to you in other ways. Sure everyone knows about karma and hopes to do the right thing so it will shine upon them but being altruistic about it for no benefit other than good intentions is a character based trait I hope I have a little of.

If you have the ability to make a different in a cause, a charity, a person's life just by doing what you do every day then give it a try. I met a young man at the ENACTUS competition, student entrepreneurs national competition in Vancouver in May. He told me he founded MealShare a non-profit to help the homeless and 'Tonight for Tomorrow' was back for its second year. He told me it was the perfect reason to eat at one of your favourite restaurants! For every dollar spent on dinner at participating restaurants on a certain day, <u>two dollars</u> would be donated to **help grow Mealshare!**

Of course, I jumped on board it took no more than a minute to copy and paste his words off the website on Facebook and Twitter and I hope that it made a difference to his campaign. Do it for goodness sake not by expecting something in return.

Solving a Problem

I think the number one reason people go on the internet is to solve an everyday problem. From finding that car dealer on 5th street that you wanted to call but forgot the name or the proper way to prune a rose to looking for a partner or booking a cruise we need the internet to solve our problems – quickly!

People appreciate you like crazy when you can solve a problem for them. It's the basis for sales and business, after all. However, there is more than one way to have social media assist you in your business, in fact, there are 30. Read on potential rock stars.

"To succeed in business it is necessary to make others see things as you see them."

Aristotle Onassis
Shipping Tycoon

Chapter 8 – 30 Ways to Use Social Media for Business

Social media by definition seems to preclude business people from using it, it's supposed to be social. But wow, what an amazing tool for business. I've used social media to sell things and ideas, to promote businesses, to change Canadian Law as an agent of change and brand myself as an international expert. The most important thing for a business owner to remember with social media is that you must ENGAGE people and continue to engage them with valuable and consistent content. What can your company do with social media? It's more a question of what can't you do with social media. Check these few points out.

1. Get Feedback

I spoke to a local high-end restaurant about comments made on Yelp, a social media site, about their menus and staff, none of which were complimentary. The manager had never heard of Yelp, or any social media platforms for that matter, but it is a great tool to get feedback on your customers experience and mitigate any negative experiences. It is absolutely imperative in todays tuned in society that every business monitors what people say about them good or bad. You know what they say; give good service and they will tell one person, give bad service and they will tell the world. Or you can simply listen to what people say on Facebook, Twitter, blogs and forums. There are a variety of tools for that.

I was having a few drinks at my local Cactus Club with a couple of friends and made a comment on Twitter that I was surprised that they had considerably raised the price of my favorite wine. When I got my bill the wine had been charged at the old price saving me about $3 a glass. The server smiled and said she thought the price was too high so she had given me a discount. These people monitored social media the entire time the restaurant was open to be able to respond to comments like mine. Wow!

2. Create Demand

What better way to create demand for your product or service than to use guerilla marketing that is free. Better than simply reacting you can proactively inform everyone about upcoming products, features or services. This way the demand is there before the actual product arrives. Apple does this all the time. With target marketing and using geocaching, you can target people near your store or business via their Smartphone GPS and offer them specials to come to your store. Some may think this is a bit intrusive but hey a deal is a deal and if it bothers you, you can turn your GPS off.

3. Offer Discounts

Speaking of geocaching, I was approaching my favorite Starbucks close to home when I got a text ad on my iPhone offering me a free donut with my coffee if I came in and tried the new coffee shop that opened just down the block. I admit I was curious and tried it out. It was nice but I was not swayed by the donut to leave my other 'office'.

Who hasn't heard of Groupon, a boon for some and a bane for others? Sure it is tempting to give away the farm for new customers figuring more will come through your door but the truth was that some business owners over extended themselves with the amazing power of Groupon discounts. Once you have an account on Facebook or Twitter or even before you gain a significant following the best thing you can do is offer discounts. People will follow you then and they also will buy. Dell has been selling computers on Twitter for years.

The best way to use discounts is to offer discounts on products or services that are not in great demand. Using Daily Deal products on your best seller is suicide for your business and needs to be avoided at all costs.

4. Get Attention

Followers on Twitter, good content on your blog, insightful comments on Facebook will get you attention. Attention is easily turned into money. When my Twitter following was around 200,000 people a Canadian government department was paying me $750 per tweet to promote their tradeshows on a quarterly basis. That government department overspent on their budget but my hyper-local tweets targeted the exact client they needed to reach in Vancouver and proved to be successful.

Sounds simple doesn't it? Say something of importance and then you might get attention. Why? Well, on the Web money is not the most valuable asset; it's attention and brand influencing. It can be turned into money but you earn more money in the long term by trying to get attention repeatedly. I've had more opportunities thrown my way via my Twitter account.

5. Spread the Word

Tell the people about you and your business once you have established a connection with your following by getting attention over and over again and again. With a following of more than half a million followers on Twitter my reach is sometimes estimated at 7.5 million. Spreading the word allows me to offer advice, change Canadian law (yes Bill C470) and influence people.

Announce changes on your blog, promote your next appearance at a conference or like mentioned above, present your new product. I find it satisfying to be able to help others in a pay it forward manner as well. If I see someone promoting a charity event or a GoFundMe campaign I'll step in to promote their cause with a few well placed/timed tweets.

6. Build Brand Loyalty

92% of people trust what friends say on social media according to Forbes. Brand loyalty is self-explanatory isn't it? People like your brand and then buy from you again in the future. How do you make them loyal customers? Either by providing formidable goods and services or you provide something for free, be it information or community. With false news and the reputation of the largest news organizations being downgraded to opinion polls we need a new alternative.

7. Establish a Community

The web is now interest based and marketers realize the old use of demographics is outdated and 'like' is not only the new buzz word but is also the norm to establish community. Imagine 'liking' to read an obscure comic or manga character and being able to setup a community on Meetup or others in order to hang with like-minded people. Very powerful stuff folks. The Web is a great place for creating communities. Why? People from all over the world that are obsessed with the same weird hobby can virtually meet with other like-minded individuals. You can establish a community of fans of your brand right there on your blog, feedback site or Facebook group. I have a fan base on Twitter but my favorite is Meetups for local in-personal gatherings.

Don't forget that when you cross-promote your Tweets to LinkedIn, Facebook and others you are building a community there as well. The same people do not hang out in those social media platforms at the same time so most of the time when you post it's to different people.

8. Answer Questions

I get huge traffic to my website and blog because I love to answer questions put forth by people on

MosaicHUB, Yahoo and others in my area of expertise, namely startups. These Ask Me Anything sessions raise your profile and send valuable traffic to wherever you want to promote. People ask questions all the time on the Web. That's why start-ups like Quora try to be the next big thing while Yahoo Answers had more traffic that Twitter up to 2013. Replay and answer questions, be helpful, whether you are dealing with your won products and services or the niche by and large. The great side benefit of answering questions on a site like Quora is that you use answers from other experts as well. I've learned lots and from differing perspectives just by reading other peoples answers.

9. Provide Support

My wife, Jo Ann, is a certified Linux expert and was trying to install a new version on my new laptop. It wouldn't work so she spent considerable time on forums until she found some help. The help was great but she had to do some more work to allow the program to be installed. She then posted the work-a-round to the same forum to help others. Sometimes people have more than questions. They are annoyed, angry or even desperate. Your product or service may have caused that suffering. I think it's also important to pay it forward whenever you can.

10. Get Clients

Of course if you are engaging people and using social media correctly you will find leads to sell your product or service. Remember to ask for the sale. Giving advice, providing needed content on your blog and websites is great but you need a call to action. I don't think getting clients is your sole action when using social media. You should always provide quality information and engage in a fundamental policy of offering solutions and advice to people first, the sales will come as a result. Don't forget there is nothing wrong with becoming known as a thought-leader or expert in your field. Tell the world!

11. Improve CRM

Does your company use customer relationship management tools like Salesforce? Well, many CRM tools already support CRM features to manage relationships beyond customers or rather before they become customers. You can view past conversations with each Twitter user you interact with. Online customer interactions with brands grew 70% between 2013 and 2014. According to McKinsey, 30% of these people prefer a direct message versus sitting on hold on a customer service line. This is understandable. After all, this is an on-demand world. Waiting around for someone to answer the phone is a thing of the past. All of your customers live on social media so you better be there too.

The three ways to use social media for your CRM are:

1. To deal with complaints. I've nailed companies online for bad customer service and the good ones have dealt decisively and quickly to my concerns –kudos to them.
2. Using social media you can move the complaint to private mode and avoid an even worse PR dilemma.
3. You can use social media to create more value in your products. There are opportunities online for you to both upsell and cross-sell your products.

Topsy is a tool find out what is trending

12. Empower Staff

I got on Twitter because a client told me about a company that gave each salesperson an iPhone then asked them to send 10 tweets about the business to the world every day. This really worked for the company and the sales guys actually enjoyed the ability to promote their employer. Imagine employees who take pride in their work and want the world to know, give them the tools to do it. I was so amazed at this 'new' technology I embraced it and became a global influencer – thank you BuildDirect.

13. Monitor Trends

#Hashtags on Twitter is an easy way to see what is trending. You can find out more on social media than just who is talking or complaining about you. Many tools allow you to watch trends unfold. You determine what's cool and where the demand is almost instantly by scanning Facebook and Twitter with simple tools like Topsy. On the other hand why not start your own trend. I can read Canadian political news by searching for #CDNpoli (Canadian Politics). I also can track my fav posts that I send out by hashtagging #BizQuotes. It allows me to search old Twitter posts, finding 'gems' and ReTweeting them to a new audience.

14. Identify Influencers

Topsy also allows you to find out who actually tweets about your business. You can check how many clicks these people brought to your site via bit.ly or Twitter's own stats. Indeed Topsy even marks important users "influential" or "highly influential" based on their activity. Just as watching trends are great for finding content, it's important that you follow influencers because they tend to be on the leading edge of their industry.

15. Reach Out

LinkedIn is particularly easy at reaching out to other business people. You can see who has checked out your profile and connect that way. Once you know who likes you, you can reach out to these people. Blogger outreach is even an established industry term by now. Contact them, simply express your gratitude, invite them to your next product presentation or send them your products for testing purposes. I like to add LION or **LinkedIn Open Networker**, after my name. To

Linked In Open Networker
LION

those in the know, it means I will follow anyone who wants to follow me. You never know who you will find in the LI database. I've amassed a fair number of followers on LI basically because I get involved and engage my followers at every opportunity be it reposting articles I've written on Equities.com or commenting on impressive posts I've read by others. I think 1/3 of my international business comes from connections I've made on LinkedIn.

16. Discuss Features

Feedback is great as long as it is constructive. Don't stifle bad comments in any medium especially your blog as it does allow you to identify problem areas and maybe sometimes allows you to change or modify existing procedures etc. which will make your customer's experience with you even better. Facebook pages are a good place for your business to find problem areas and to fix them. Others will see that you are a conscientious business and appreciate that you work with customer service. I draw the line on personal attacks but it is amazing to me that those who do give you a hard time will apologize once you have acknowledged it and respond to them.

17. Facilitate Testing

Social sites are not only for chatting aka conversation. Some sites like <u>Clue</u> e.g. offer user testing as a free service. Usability testing is not only a task for experts you always need real people do the testing as well. Approach them on social media and simply ask to perform a short test. I use people as feedback on any number of issues and people are more than willing to help. I've asked for help in an issue regarding my crappy Pioneer receiver in my bedroom to choosing a new vehicle.

18. Debunk Myths

MacDonald's took to YouTube to tell people in an amusing way that their Chicken McNuggets were not made with chicken lips and beaks but with real white breast meat. Still not sure if I believe them but they did address the story that was going around the web. People may misunderstand your product or have had a bad experience. You can counter these allegations with numbers, customer feedback, etc. Often people complain about your brand even without trying it just because someone else said, "it sucks". In this era of #alternatenews and the big news channels offering opinion versus news telling the truth is more important than ever.

19. Market Offerings

Yes, indeed, you can market your offerings as well. It's not like marketing elsewhere though. You don't appear on the social media scene and start shouting about you and your offers. All the actions mentioned above and below are <u>part</u> of your marketing. People like you when you do all of or at least part of it right and then nobody will be mad at you for just mentioning your offer even without it being new or a bargain. If you try to sell something to people on social media make sure you have something to give them as well. Give them a free article or whitepaper and they will buy your products. I really, really try not to make it appear that I am trying to sell my followers something. On the other hand if I recommend a product or service I am using all is forgiven.

20. Forge Relationships

People hate talking to the anonymous support people (usually in another country) on the phone. They want to deal with real people. My telephone company in Canada allows me to connect with a real person through chat who has a name, is friendly and they make you feel like you are talking to a friend. I've made some very interesting friends on social media. I've engaged with them, listened to their stories and offered help when I can. A couple of minutes helping someone find a solution to a serious problem to me is paying it forward. I freely offer my email to anyone on social media to connect. You never know what is coming down the pipe and I certainly have time to listen.

21. Develop Authority

A real life person telling the truth, being helpful and sharing valuable information more than once is on her or his way to develop authority. Isn't it logical? So having a recognizable representative over time can make your company exec or spokesperson become an industry authority important beyond the position s/he has in your company. Becoming an influencer by definition is an amazing accomplishment. Influencers are made not born and to be able to provide expert and valid opinions to those who are looking for it is very rewarding. This is a sure method to make cash from your experience. Why shop anywhere else if you can buy it from the expert?

22. Build Links

Building links for your company blog is an easy and effective way to manage your SEO. Social media allows you to join various platforms and have your link in your profile. There's nothing wrong with putting your business link in your twitter post or other posts and direct people back to a point you are making in your blog. Every post, be it a blog or Twitter, provides you with the opportunity to put your name in the forefront and promote your service or product. A link costs nothing and bothers no one.

23. Raise Funds

Social media is an excellent fundraising tool. Crowdfunding is the new way to raise capital outside the typical startup route. Typically the funding is lower than traditional methods but is effective for its speed of raising funds and the promotional value it delivers to those seeking funds. Kickstarter and Indiegogo are the two biggest and best-known crowdfunding platforms. I've used both platforms and find that another option Equity Crowdfunding is a better model. It allows you to give 'investors' a small piece of your business making them part of the solution. I've noticed also that on the crowdfunding side if you don't have a tech company you are promoting with some cool gadgets then you are trying to climb a very slippery slope. People want a story or a new product they can get behind. Early adopters tend to be the perfect customer so they want to be wowed.

24. Get Publicity

This is different than getting attention. Think of social media when you want to issue that press release or news of an event or promotion. Soon after I published my book, "How to Start a Successful Business – the First Time" on Amazon, I got my first speaking engagement at a national conference on entrepreneurs for thousands of dollars. They would not have hired me without my online press release about the book. Social

Google Alerts says what is happening in your industry

Media is about information processing and anything relevant to other people that you want to release is not only fair but it is necessary.

25. Watch the Competition

Internet marketers spend a lot of time watching the competition on social media. They learn from them in terms of what to do and what not to do. It is very valuable to know what is trending in your industry and know when to make changes to your brand by watching others. Google Alerts is a good resource but plenty of other tools assist you here. The cool thing about a small company is that by watching others you can pivot your product or service a lot more effectively and efficiently that the big guys who need corporate approval to make changes to their core offerings.

26. Find Talent

Does anyone hire headhunters anymore to find employees? Of course they do but LinkedIn is a great resource to find talent because latest figures from the Forrest Group indicate that 85% of all recruiters are on LinkedIn watching and looking for talented individuals

Earl Flormata

to hire. I have several hundred recruiters following me on LinkedIn. I'm thinking if that incredible CEO job for Apple comes up they might call but I won't hold my breath. Every designer, programmer, partner I've ever worked with have come from being on social media.

27. Organize

Using social media you can organize people all over the world to work with you. You can set up user groups in any country in the world; have beta testers and beta users anywhere through social media. My friend and buddy, Earl Flormata is called the Evil Marketing Genius for a good reason – he has tapped the outsourcing marketing in the Philippines to do everything from virtual assistant to programming for him at a greatly reduced rate. I've taken his lead and regularly work with his team in the Philippines and a custom marketing firm in Malta filled with expat Irish guys owned by a friend of mine in Vancouver – sweet! The sweet thing is that the Philippines is about 13 hours behind me and Malta is 9 hours the other way so while I'm sleeping someone is working for me.

I was with a friend the other day and I mentioned how I

have several hundred business cards that I had in a pile in my office that I needed to do something with. She laughed and said her virtual assistant does all that stuff. She was actually amused when she told me her VA charges her $4 an hour and works about 20 hours a week for her. Again, with the VA in Pakistan, my friend leaves for the day at work and the VA's work is ready for her in the morning.

28. Create Value

Real value today is in data and knowledge. By sharing valuable information your company gets a reputation for this and it will come back to you in client acquisition or retention. Much of my day is spent researching the Internet whether it is for an article I'm writing or a company I am working with to raise funds. If you give me good material I will be your pal forever.

You will see a lot of companies offering white papers on a particularly interesting or needed topic. Sure they are creating value but the reason they do this is to capture your email address. Everyone knows what they are doing but the content is so good we give them the email anyway. Hootsuite is really good at this and I love their ten page white papers.

29. Locate Markets

On social media you have people from all over the world listening. When your market is crowded you can discover another market somewhere else. I find it fascinating when I see a product in Canada that never sold at home but is a big item in Europe. Think outside the box and find your own market niche in other international markets. It's all possible on social media.

30. Meet Peers

I love watching my peers (and enemies) and keeping them close. Can you imagine a time in the past when 5 t-shirt companies could share a common office? There is no competition on the Internet because there is enough to go around. Sharing best practices supports the community and everyone wins.

Earl Flormata literally told me he has used systems and programs to manage his social media and office systems for a simple reason – he is lazy. I try to keep my social media

simple but there are many programs available to the little guy to manage social media and other functions related to social media platforms. Consider them add-ons to any social platform.

The big guys, like Joe Fresh, Starbucks, LuLu Lemon use the same platforms you and I do - Twitter, Facebook, Google+, etc.— but their marketing plans and their marketing tools are likely quite different. Enterprise solutions are great for the big guys, but the rest of us are in the market for something more our size.

Small businesses must find tools that take a lot of the time and trouble out of social media marketing and that do so without costing an arm and a leg. I'm a guerilla marketer meaning I love using free or very inexpensive online tools so most of the time I know I am getting good return on my "free" investment of only my time (yes, time is money). But how do you know you are really getting a good ROI return on investment for your time?

"Do one thing every day that scares you."

Eleanor Roosevelt
First Lady to 32nd US President

Do one thing every day that scares you
Eleanor Roosevelt

Chapter 9 – Social Media's Return on Investment (ROI)

The companies that hire me for social media campaigns have the information about my social media that they know fits into their target audience. They know that my Twitter demographics are mainly males (64%) between 32 to 52 years. They know my followers are mainly entrepreneurs (73%) who love premium brands and earn around $200,000 a year. They know that 70% own their own home and 54% are married. They know all this because of the analytics they use and the research they pay for that allows them to find people like me to advertise for them.

Big companies know exactly how much money they need to

spend to get one customer and you would be surprised how high that is in some cases. That is the reason many companies have customer retention departments to talk you out of leaving because it costs so much to get you as a customer in the first place when you consider people, television, marketing department etc. to capture you.

It makes sense for Microsoft or PayPal to pay me $300US for a Tweet when they may get 500 hot prospects from the engagement I offer.

For you to do a campaign on Facebook you may think the only way to measure the success of your ad campaign is through adding up your sales at the end of the month. You couldn't be further from the truth because there are 'hidden' benefits from everything you do on social media.

10 Value-added ROI's from Social Media

1. Your Reputation

Everything you do on social media from tweeting while drinking your chardonnay to posting photos on Facebook or Instagram tell people about you and your business. I had someone comment on my 11:30 am

lunch photo I posted on Instagram like I see my friends do. I took a nice photo of a beautifully prepared and presented cooked halibut with fries. Innocuous enough until the person commented to me on Instagram that it was kind of early to be drinking alcohol – what? When I looked at the photo there was a glass of chardonnay in the top left corner of the picture.

Not everyone is liberal enough to think that having a glass of wine at lunch is a good thing. After responding politely to the person on Instagram I realized many people saw my silly picture and I wondered how many felt the way the person did? The old adage if you have one disgruntled customer they tell ten friends yet a happy customer will tell no one came to mind.

Your reputation is everything and you must protect it at all costs.

2. Reducing Risk

I've mentioned before in this book about the restaurateur who didn't know what people were saying about his establishment because he didn't use

Yelp or any social media for that matter. Aghg, when will people learn that you need to know what is happening in your community? Being engaged with your customers and knowing their needs is the best ROI.

3. Customer Retention

Going hand in hand with reducing risk, customer retention is an easy one to manage. Assuming you offer a great product or service and your customer experience is wonderful then the world is good to you. However, as we all know sometimes glitches happen, a parcel is late, we have a bad day and are not as attentive as we should or a lock of the chef's hair suddenly appeared on someone's hamburger.

If you are on top of social media and your brand you will know issues as they arise, problems and how to fix them and ways to improve things because of customer feedback. If you monitor the activities of your customer you can offer advice, solutions or even give them connections.

I was buying a sign the other day and asked the sign maker about those cool standup banners. He told me

Alignable to find a sign maker

he didn't make them but gave me the name and number of a competitor who did. Guess what? I like that and will go back to the first guy the next time I need something. As it turned out I asked him to order it for me through his company so he would get kudos from the competition. When the banner came it was the same price as if I had gone to the competitor because my guy ordered it wholesale – very cool networking.

4. Finding Suppliers

ROI can be finding great suppliers you normally would not have found just be using social media to ask other people who they use. I found my sign/banner maker on **Alignable** after we connected and thought I'd try him out. The recommendations and testimonials on his profile told me what I need to know about him and his customer service.

5. Public Exposure

By developing a good social media following and representing your business in the best light is a public relations blessing. Being a social media influencer will send a lot of people to your door among them will be customers. Your buzz will impact others and attract the right kind of clients to you, those that allow you to pick and choose the ones you want to work with instead of taking everyone that offers you money.

6. Brand Association

Collectively all of your social media will identify your brand. If you mess up on some key messaging you may lose your reputation and all that you have worked for. On the other hand, if you have defined your brand in your mind and are using the same messaging across all of your social media platforms you will come out ahead. With a good social media following you won't need to spend bucks on Facebook or Goggle ads because people are following you and listening to your pitches from your social media posts.

7. Immediate Revenue

It may seem obvious but the more traffic you can attract will gain you more revenue. IF you have a large following on social media your followers are free. This is not to say that you abuse them but since they are following you, you can pitch them ideas and gather opportunities at will without selling to them. The more active you are the more opportunities will come your way.

8. Long Term Revenue

When you have great content on Twitter and other social media sites people become fans. Fans become customers and if you are good to them they become advocates. Advocates provide great promotional material in the form of ReTweets, forwarded posts and links to your websites. Any time you can from a relationship with a customer they become advocates and will tell others about your great product or service. Keep them in mind when you are giving out bonuses.

9. Business Intelligence

Business intelligence on social media is like sleuthing or being a private eye. IT give you the ability to listen to everyone in your industry and engage with them. On social media you can access any company or industry and use what you find to tailor your own social media campaign to focus on their weaknesses and flaws.

10. Differentiation

The level of your engagement on social media may differentiate you from your competitors. If you follow your clients or prospective clients you will find out a lot about them and you will be able to refer to this information in social media posts or Tweets to them.

In many cases the only differentiator between you and your competitors is a meaningful relationship. Relationships are easily engaged and maintained using social media. What part of 'social' is hard to understand? Just jump in

Now that you know how to achieve return on investment, for your social media, time to learn about the technology tools you can leverage to manage it, track it and ensure you have great content.

> *"I have not failed.
> I've just found 10,000 ways that won't work"*
>
>
>
> **Thomas A. Edison**
> Extraordinary Inventor

Chapter 10 – Social Media Tools for Small Business

I've been referred to a great deal of programs over the past couple of years and while I don't claim to use most of them I've heard good things about them so they are worth the effort to check out. Hopefully you find one or two here that you can use in your small-scale marketing that can get you big results. I didn't want to bore you and have you flip past all these cool tools but skim carefully if you must and pick up a few treasures.

Don't get overwhelmed! Just try a few that appeal. I have put stars by my current personal favorites.

Dashboards / Management Tools

Nuvi

Used by brands like Uber, Chevron, Nissan, and more, Nuvi is a social media marketing suite that is unique in its stunning social media data visualizations. Nuvi simplifies social media data reporting and monitoring, so marketers can focus on shaping their social media strategy.

Edgar

Edgar flips content scheduling on its head by scheduling content by categories. Once all the new content in a category has been shared, Edgar recycles older updates to maintain engagement and widen social reach.

Post Planner

Post Planner claims to apply science to social media and content to identify the best content for your audience. Users can browse Post Planner's recommended feeds to discover new content, and its algorithms measure data from previous posts to predict future engagement and help shape social strategy.

CoSchedule

Though CoSchedule is actually a full-fledged marketing

calendar, it's a great choice for social media marketers as well. By linking all of your platforms and managing them from CoSchedule, you're able to plan, promote, and execute your entire strategy from a single tool.

Sprout Social

Sprout Social is a social media management platform that features a Unified Smart Inbox to streamline social engagement. It also offers customer support features like tasks and Helpdesk, and team collaboration tools like live activity updates.

Later

Later is the quintessential Instagram post scheduling app, used by brands like GQ, Yelp, and The Huffington Post. Later features an intuitive calendar view, bulk uploading, and a search function that makes it easy for Instagram marketers to find and repost engaging content.

Respond

Respond is another tool from the Buffer team. It's a software platform that links social media and customer support. It turns mentions, direct messages, and searches into tickets that reside in a single inbox, making it simple to consolidate customer service efforts.

Tweetdeck

Tweetdeck, now owned by Twitter, is a simple and fully-featured customizable dashboard for Twitter. It organizes feeds, notifications, messages and more using an easy-to-follow column view, and supports management of multiple accounts, making it perfect for the social media marketing enthusiast. You can quickly see at-a-glance the activity from different lists, followers, hashtags, and more. I'd hate for my friends at Hootsuite to read this but I prefer Tweetdeck.

SocialBro

Social Bro can tell you everything you want to know about your Twitter account—community information, analytics on all your posts, and much more. There is a 15-day free trial to test out all the features. The community insights are fascinating, and there's great tweet analytics which show you which posts got the most engagement and when.

Tweet Jukebox

Tweet Jukebox, which lets you schedule multiple Tweets throughout the day or week, solving the problem of getting content out there. Tweet Jukebox acts like the old time record jukeboxes but with Tweets. You preload it, and then leave it to Tweet for you at specified times and days of the week. On Friday, Tweet Jukebox will automatically thank the people who mentioned you on Twitter during the week.

Tweetcaster

This is a Twitter management tool for iOS and Android devices, and it provides the basics of what you'd expect from a Twitter dashboard plus a few fun extras: enhanced search and lists, hiding unwanted tweets, and photo effects for your pics. Put this tool to use: Keep the app on the first screen of your phone and tablet so you can easily dip in and out of your Twitter streams when time allows. With ten million users the company calls it "the best thing to happen to Twitter since Twitter".

Followerwonk

This is one of my favorite ways to analyze and optimize our Twitter accounts at Buffer. With Followerwonk, you can do all sorts of amazingly helpful things like analyze your Twitter followers, compare different users, and search through bios—all for free. There are even more features—like tracking and sorting your followers—that you can access with a 30-day trial. This will allow you to dig really deep into twitter analytics.

Social Rank

This Twitter tool identifies your top 10 followers in three specific areas: Best Followers, Most Engaged, and Most Valuable. Your engaged followers are those who interact with you most often (replies, retweets, and favorites), your most valuable followers are the influential accounts, and your best followers are a combination of the two. Social Rank will run the numbers for free and show you the results today then follow-up each month with an email report.

ManageFlitter

The Twitter tool helps you filter whom you follow: Easily unfollow those who don't follow you back, those who've never changed their profile photo, and those who are inactive. One of their tools is PowerPost that has a unique interface that allows you to quickly see the best time to post Tweets based on your account.

Must Be Present

Searches your Twitter account to find how quickly you respond to mentions. Their engagement reports place you in a percentile based on other accounts so you can see how you stack up to the speed of others. Aim for a certain percentile or a particular average response time. Customers engaging with brands on this app increased 178% in 2013. That's nine times

Tweepi = optimization of followers

the growth rate of the social networks themselves.

Tweriod

Tells you when you'll receive the most exposure for your tweets by analyze your account. The Tweriod reports break it down into daily and hourly windows when you can expect the highest engagement with what you share.

Tweepi

Tweepi manages your followers, and supercharging who you're following. For management, you can unfollow in batches those who don't follow you back, and you can bulk follow another account's complete list of followers or who they're following. You can bulk edit your connections on Twitter. Tweriod gives you the best times to tweet. They analyze both your tweets and your followers' tweets. So you can start tweeting when it makes most sense to reach others.

Tweet4me

Teet4me can schedule your Tweets. Once you're signed up with Tweet4me, you can send them a direct message that contains a certain prefix, containing information on when and what to post. Sign-up and send them a Direct Message with a prefix that tells Tweet4me when you want to schedule the Tweet. They schedule the tweet and when the time comes,

[handwritten note at top: dlvr.it = Jules best stuff to re-tweet]

we'll post it for you and send you a push notification via Boxcar.

Commun.it

This app can help you organize, grow, and manage your followers, and it can do so across multiple accounts and profiles. At-a-glance, you can see different parts of your community management, like latest tweets from your stream and which new followers might appreciate a welcome. Listen to Commun.it's advice on the most influential accounts around your brand. It allows you to prioritize your feed, manage followers, engage your followers and points out some high-value influencers.

Twtrland

Now called Klear, it gives you a snapshot of your Twitter profile and can track Facebook and Instagram for you as well. Two of Twtrland's most helpful tools are a live count of how many followers are currently online and advanced search functionality that includes keywords, locations, and companies. Find Influencers in any skill, location in the world. Covering 500M profiles across all networks.

dlvr.it

Smart Social Media Automation, The easiest way to find and

share great content to Facebook, Twitter, Pinterest and more.

TweetReach

This Twitter tool shows you the reach and exposure of the tweets you send, collecting data on who ReTweets you and the influence of each. It is now a piece of Union Metrics that is more than free TweetReach snapshot reports! We've upgraded TweetReach Pro and it's now part of Union Metrics subscriptions. Monitor all the topics and profiles important to you on Twitter, Instagram and Facebook. Improve your social media strategy and execution across social media with Union Metrics.

Twazzup

Offers real-time monitoring and analytics for Twitter on any name, keyword, or hashtag you choose. The Twazzup results page delivers interesting insights like who the top influencers are for your keyword and which top links are associated with your search. Check out the links and influencers associated with your name.

Buffer

Buffer builds a queue of the content and sends it out on a regular schedule to your various timelines. It's simple and easy. Save time managing your social media Schedule, publish and analyze all your posts in one place.

Social Media Analytics Tools

LikeAlyzer

This Facebook analysis tool comes up with stats and insights into your page and starts off every report with a list of recommendations. Keep track of where you stand compared to other pages by following the comparison of your page to average page rank, industry-specific page rank, and the rank of similar brands.

Fanpage Karma

It shows all sorts of valuable info related to your Facebook page like growth, engagement, service and response time, and of course Karma (a weighted engagement value). It let's you analyze your profiles - and your competitors. With KPIs, analyses and reports. Monitor your success and increase your social reach every day.

Audiense

Audiense (formerly SocialBro) is a tool that provides a wealth of social media insights. It helps marketers create segments, understand audience behavior, optimize engagement, and track and report both organic and paid campaigns in detail.

Mention

Mention is one of the best ways to monitor your brand across the web and social media. It monitors a multitude of channels in real time to provide users with live updates about their brands, and features competitive analysis, influencer finding, and automated reports.

Klear

Klear is a social intelligence platform that helps users improve their social media marketing efforts by offering monitoring and reporting tools, influencer search, and social profile analysis. It also features a built-in "mini influencer CRM" that allows users to connect with influencers efficiently.

Keyhole

The tracking tool keeps track of your hashtag campaign or keyword on Twitter, Instagram, or Facebook with a full dashboard of analytics, demographics, and influencers. Start a hashtag around an upcoming event, and keep track of the popularity of the tag before, during, and after.

Crowdfire

Crowdfire is a social media management tool that allows you to manage followers on Twitter and Instagram. It provides insight into people who follow you, people who don't, and finding inactive or influential users. It's the ideal tool for maximizing the relevance and engagement of your followers on social media. You can follow targeted people or use keywords to find like-minded people to follow.

Instagram for Business

Instagram for Business is a feature within Instagram that allows brands to turn their accounts into Business accounts. This unlocks a "contact" button, business insights, and the ability to create ads and promote posts directly within the Instagram app.

Iconosquare

Iconosquare is an analytics and marketing suite for Instagram, and is used by brands including H&M, National Geographic, MTV, and more. It provides insights like follower analytics and engagement, Instagram post scheduling for multiple accounts, and photo and video contests.

SocialRank

SocialRank is a tool that assists users in identifying, organizing, and managing followers on Twitter and Instagram.

It features follower sorting and filtering to help brands identify their most influential and most engaged followers.

Facebook Insights

Though Insights is just a feature built into Facebook's Pages, it's a tool that provides a wealth of analytics that are valuable to any marketer. In addition to showcasing impressions and engagement, Insights can be exported for further analysis.

Engage by Twitter

Engage is a Twitter companion app for iOS that helps Twitter users grow and understand their Twitter audiences by analyzing real-time data to generate insights. It also features monetization options so influencers and brands can drive revenue through the platform.

#BePresent

#BePresent is an "experiment in social brand engagement" by Sprout Social. What does this mean for marketers? A free report highlighting your brand's engagement on social media, including average response times and rates compared to other brands.

Rival IQ

Rival IQ tracks a list of brands of your choosing and monitors their activity on Facebook, Twitter, Google+, LinkedIn, and even SEO. Your free 14-day trial gives you full access to competitor tracking and the dashboards for each of the different networks and search factors.

Nuzzel

Nuzzel is a news-reading app that created a feed based on what friends are reading and sharing. This results in a feed with topics closely related to your interests and allows you to find prime content to share on social.

Feedly

Feedly is the news-reader most of the content team uses here at Wishpond. Users can create and customize feeds based on their interests, and assigns each post a "heat score" that determines its engagement – making it a cinch to find out what's hot and what's not.

Quuu.co

Content curating is one of the most difficult parts of social media marketing – it can be tough to know what your audiences will like. Quuu takes the work out of curating by hand-curating content for you based on your audience's interests that gets send to your Buffer account immediately.

Buzz Sumo

Buzz Sumo finds the best content on each topic

~~Wonder~~ what the most popular content is on any given topic or any particular website? It has this covered with a search tool that tracks content and ranks according to shares on Facebook, Twitter, LinkedIn, Google+, and Pinterest.

Klout

This is one of the more well-known tools on this list. I like this program a lot. It gives me some great analytics. It collects information on a person's various social profiles to come up with a popularity score of 1 to 100 and then lets you follow your score over time as it ebbs and flows (ideally flowing upward). You can track topics, view content suggestions, and post straight to your connected social profiles. Mine is around 75 so it could use improvement.

SharedCount

There will be times when you'll need/want to know how popular your content is. SharedCount shows you quickly, at a glance, how far and wide a piece of content spread. Use the dashboard to see a table of multiple URLs for a week's worth of content.

Google URL Builder

If you're dabbling in advanced campaign tracking, you've

> UTM codes at the end of a URL that show traffic

likely read up on UTM tracking codes in links. A UTM code is basically extra characters at the end of a link that help flesh out your analytics reports, showing you where your traffic came from and what campaigns it's all associated with.

Visual Content Tools

Pablo

Pablo is another visual media tool, created by Buffer, With over 50,000 images and a simple drag and drop editor with over 25 fonts, Pablo is one of the easiest ways to create engaging images in different sizes for every social network. Pablo even features several filters to make your images stand out.

Pexels

When you're looking to create visual media to share on your social platforms, Pexels is the perfect place to find free, beautiful stock images. The site searches a multitude of stock image sites so you're always sure to find the images you're looking for.

Pablo looks like a great visual tool

Easelly

Easelly is a tool that simplifies making infographics, which is important when you consider the impact of visual media on engagement. With its large library of templates, marketers are sure to find an infographic outline that suits their needs.

Adobe Spark

Easelly = Infographic tool

Spark is a web-based tool from Adobe that turns ideas into graphics, web stories, and animated videos. It simplifies these processes making it simple for creatives and non-creatives alike to create beautiful, engaging media in minutes for sharing on social channels. Spark also features three iOS apps so you can create on the go.

quickmeme

Love 'em or hate 'em, memes are some of the most viral content on social media. quickmeme provides meme templates that users can add text to, making it easy to share funny, captioned pictures of cats, or babies, or whatever.

GIPHY

Giphy = Moving images

GIFs have become an integral part of the social media experience – they're everywhere. GIPHY is the web's largest GIF database, containing all of the moving images you'll ever need for sharing with your social media following.

Pexels = Stock Images

Infogr.am

This one helps you build sparkling infographics by entering information right into the Infogram spreadsheets that are built right in to the editor. Standard features are there, too, like design templates and a full design editor. This will give you visual content plus transparency.

Piktochart

This is a free-to-try infographic creator with a full editor and themes to turn your data into a work of art. They say their designers work hard so you don't have to. In fact, you'll have access to a weekly updated library of over **600** professionally-designed templates. Finding a style that fits your message is easy.

Canva

The graphic design app has an incredibly intuitive drag-and-drop interface, and the tooltips and templates make it ideal for beginner designers. Everything is free unless you choose to use something from Canva's library of stock photos. I think this is one of the most popular programs with about 10 million users you can't go wrong.

Compfight

Compfight is an image search engine tailored to efficiently

Compfight finds the right images

locate images for blogs, comps, inspiration, and research. We make good use of the flickr™ API, but aren't affiliated with flickr. This app is my source for creative commons images to accompany our content. For your social media posts, images like these can be great additions to a visual content strategy (just be sure to give credit where credit's due—each compfight picture comes with attribution). Build a small library of free-to-use photos for upcoming social sharing.

BeFunky

Images + Cropping

This one is one of the best graphics program and easiest— ones around, with a complete suite of image editing tools like cropping, scaling, filters, text, and more.

Visual content like this is ideal for social networks, and you can pull this off easily

LICEcap

Who doesn't love GIFs? If your social media presence is strong on a place like Tumblr or Google+, then having GIF-making capabilities can come in handy. LICEcap is a downloadable program that creates GIFs from what you see on your screen.

Social Media Monitoring Tools

Mention

A good problem to have is when it becomes difficult to keep track of all the different places you are mentioned on social media. Mention prides itself on "going beyond Google Alerts" to track absolutely anywhere that your name or your company could be mentioned online.

Perch

Replaced the popular program NutShellMail. It can be difficult to know how to get the most from your social media. Every day, Perch sifts through the social media activities of over half a million small businesses and they see what works. Perch is designed to help you build better social media habits, starting from day one. Consumers interact with small businesses all over the web. Perch makes it easier to keep track of Facebook, Instagram, Google, Yelp, Twitter, and Foursquare activity with their award-winning mobile app.

SocialMention

As a tracking tool, this one has some neat bonus insights beyond their in-depth keyword tracking. SocialMention tracks areas like sentiment, passion, reach, and strength to not just

Lucky Orange makes creating visitor database easy.

tell you what's being said about your search but how those reactions feel. While you track your brand or yourself, you can also see how your sentiment changes over time. Are your mentions positive or negative? And how will this change from month to month and week to week? Type your name into this one and find yourself all over the globe – phew!

Social Media Content Tools

Lucky Orange

Lucky Orange will automatically create a recording of every visitor to your website. Quickly filter and segment recordings so you can see exactly why visitors are not converting.

Out-of-the-box, Lucky Orange successfully records dynamic and member's only pages, including even the most advanced sites and single page apps.

Digg (formerly News.me)
This app contains the top five stories shared by your networks

on Twitter and Facebook. Check what your networks are most interested in, then respond right away.

Feedly

Is one of the best RSS services out there because it does all the basics of RSS well (feed organization, display, etc.) and innovates with some really helpful new features. It works on all devices. It gives you content that you scan use in your research or business.

Pocket

You can grab the content on your social networks that looks good to you and read it later in a stripped down, easy-on-the-eyes view. Send favorite stories straight from Pocket to Twitter. Pocket (Read It Later, Inc) was founded in 2007 by Nate Weiner to help people save interesting articles, videos and more from the web for later enjoyment. Once saved to Pocket, the list of content is visible on any device — phone, tablet or computer. It can be viewed while waiting in line, on the couch, during commutes or travel — even offline. The world's leading save-for-later service currently has more than 22 million registered users and is integrated into more than 1500 apps including Flipboard, Twitter and Zite. It is available for major devices and platforms including iPad, iPhone, Android, Mac, Kindle Fire, Kobo, Google Chrome, Safari, Firefox, Opera and Windows.

Paper.li is a newspaper of interesting articles.

Paper.li

This is a fun one, it lets you create a daily newspaper of your favorite tweets and stories and share this paper with your followers. Create an industry-specific daily or weekly newspaper, and take advantage of the extra opportunity to connect with and recognize some of your influencers.

Swayy

Can be a helpful tool for finding stories for basic content based on your interests, as determined by the stuff you've shared before. Connect your Twitter or Facebook account for free, and Swayy will check your audience for the type of content they might like best and make suggestions based on its findings. Put this tool to use: Sharing interesting content on social media is a great way to build your authority and expertise on a topic. Customize Swayy's suggested topic matches so that you get only the most accurate suggestions.

Miscellaneous Tools

Flare

Flare is a social share plugin for WordPress sites and part of an overall website-boosting suite of products delivered through the Filament plugin. Filament allows you to drag and drop your social share buttons wherever you'd like on your site. Put this tool to use: Find the place that makes the most sense for your share buttons—sidebar, header, footer, etc.—and fix it up easily.

FiveHundredPlus

You can place your LinkedIn contacts into different columns for weekly, monthly, quarterly, or annual reminders to get in touch with your contacts. Place your key influencers into a monthly column so that you can be reminded to stay in regular contact.

Rapportive

You can get a lot of information on each of your email contacts, including the social accounts they're connected with and where they're employed. Currently Rapportive works only with Gmail. When you make a connection with a new person over email, Rapportive can show you how to followup for connections on their various social networks.

Bitly

Shortening a URL on Twitter can be a must as you try to squeeze inside the 140-character limit. Bitly is one of the original link shorteners. Bitly will get you a full history of the link's performance as well as an overview of all the links you've ever shared. Consider cleaning up some long or ugly URLs when you're posting to Facebook, LinkedIn, or Google+ or even when you're writing an ebook or email.

Rev

This app is a complete transcription and translation service that can help convert your audio or your English into the format and language you need. If you conduct interviews of your customers, you can use Rev to convert the audio to text for easier assimilation into marketing personas or social media profiles.

ShareRoot Board Cover Creator

ShareRoot has a handful of tools that are specific for boosting Pinterest engagement, promotion, and measuring. Some tools are inactive or under development, but one that is live now is a Pinterest Board Cover Creator that lets you create images to use as the cover for your different pin boards.

Jelly

It's billed as a social search engine—you ask questions with photos, maps, and friends and get the answers from people who know best. For instance, show folks your location and get recommendations from locals on where to eat.

This gives brands an extra opportunity to connect and add value where their customers spend their time.

SteadyDemand's tool

For an overview of the health of your Google+ page, you can use This tool to investigate what's working and what's not. The tool couldn't be simpler: Just input the URL of your company's Google+ page and then see the report on all your page activity.

Powtoon

If videos are a part of your social media this one can be a free way to test and see if it might work for you. With Powtoon, you can create and edit video clips and upload straight to YouTube. Put together a product demo for what you sell, and share this on social media to give people a visual demonstration of what your business is about.

CardMunch

This free iOS app has you take a picture of a business card

and then stores the information into your contacts and finds the person on LinkedIn. It is now linked to EVernote which took some of the kinks out of it. Good for events where you collect a large number of business cards. Scan the business cards of new contacts you meet and quickly see on LinkedIn which connections you have in common.

IFTTT

Social is just a small part of what IFTTT can do. The Internet automation app can do everything from text you tomorrow's weather to automatically update your Twitter with your Instagram photos. IFTTT connects with more than 90 channels, including Twitter, Facebook, LinkedIn, and Instagram.

Zapier

This is a bigger version of IFTTT—more channels to connect but not quite free. You do get to create five free recipes before upgrading, so you can try out Zapier with tools like MailChimp and Disqus and 250 more. Connect your email campaigns with your social accounts, sending links to your campaigns as tweets, posts, or Buffers to all your favorite social places.

GroupTweet

A great way to allow multiple people to seamlessly Tweet from a Twitter account without sharing the password.☐It's great, because it allows our employees to Tweet from the company account simply by sending a DM to the company account or adding a hashtag to their Tweets. Employees love it because they can continue to use Twitter for iPhone or Tweetbot instead of having to log into some cumbersome and

Hootsuite

Hootsuite for managing and scheduling social media posts. Even the free version Is very robust! It's great for managing multiple platforms and scheduling posts (from Vancouver, my home town).

fanpoint

A place where you can create, manage and analyze Social Media Campaigns.

CrowdBooster

Crowdbooster measures and optimizes your social media marketing, providing powerful, easy-to-use analytics and recommendations on Twitter and Facebook.

Brandgauge

Is for monitoring social media metrics. You can also cross analyze social data such number of Facebook Likes/Tweets a certain YouTube clip has. It's also free!

Flashissue

This is for Gmail users there's for creating rapid email newsletters from online

Tagboard

It creates a "bulletin board" of tweets based on hashtags in real time -- it's really cool!

Linktotweet

Get the full control over your twitter messages that you can easily embed and share directly in your application.

SproutSocial

Facebook/Twitter/GooglePlus/Analytics/etc. Very nice social media management tools.

Mrsocial

Includes monitoring, listening, engagement workflow, social media analytics and social media lead generation.

Socialdraft

It is the Social Calendar that allows you to drag and drop all your posts, schedule them and visualize what your month looks like. It's perfect for the social media maven who wants to schedule 10, 20, 100 posts over the course of next few weeks.

VideoScribe

A great tool for people making videos, content or presentations and whiteboard style animations.

Wishpond

Aha! Wishpond is a great tool for social media marketers looking to increase engagement. Its social media contest tool is a foolproof way to reach more potential customers through social to skyrocket lead generation.

Typeform

Typeform is a free and easy-to-use tool that helps you create forms and quizzes. If you're looking to create a simple and gorgeous form to get information from your social media followers, you'd be hard-pressed to find a better tool than Typeform.

Twitpress

Turns slides into GIF

I just started using which helps to extend the Twitter beyond 140 characters. http://talltweets.com/ is another tool which converts the long tweet into an image and tweets.

Facebook Live

2016 saw the widespread rise of live video, thanks in large part to Periscope, and of course, Facebook Live. New content forms are always a good thing in social media, and live video is no exception. Facebook Live allows individuals and brands alike to connect with their audiences on a much deeper level.

Click to Tweet

Click to Tweet simplifies the task of promoting, sharing and tracking content on Twitter. Users write the message they want others to share and Click to Tweet generates a link that can be shared. This link automatically posts a Tweet and can be tracked.

Curalate

Curalate (formerly Like2Buy) allows marketers to make their Instagram feeds more interactive by linking photos to other locations. This makes it easy for followers to (for example) find product pages to shop for featured items.

Have2HaveIt

Have2HaveIt is another Instagram platform that lets brands to make their feeds shoppable. Though the tool only allows users to link to one location per Instagram post, it provides analytics and customer data that makes it easier to shape marketing strategies.

Yotpo

Yotpo is a marketing tool that focuses on generating real reviews for brands, with the goal of increasing brand equity and collecting user-generated content. The product is constantly introducing new features, including one that turns user-generated content and reviews into Instagram ads.

Proofhub

Check out Proofhub! Very effective and efficient project management tool. Helps manage teams as well as clients.

Don't get too caught up in all the apps available. Find a couple that work for you and stick to them!

Chapter 11 – Raise Your Game in Social Media Marketing

We call the marketing landscape one of two things, Inbound (Pull - mostly the internet) or Outbound (Push) marketing. You be the judge of what would be more effective for your business.

Outbound Marketing (Push Marketing)

Let's assume that Outbound refers to any form of advertising we generally used prior to the Internet. The comparison is black and white.

1. Communication is pushed upon your prospective customer.

2. You give them an ad or a brochure but there is little of value coming from you; just the hope people will buy from you.
3. You don't educate, engage or entertain people.
4. The marketers had a mission to 'find the customer' al all costs.
5. Customer engagement is based on demographics which while good in itself is not as fine-tuned as the behavioral inbound approach.
6. Measurement for success of the marketing campaign was third-party data and intuitive decisions not factual.

Those poor Out-bounders are facing some tough statistics. Hundreds of millions of people in Canada and the US have registered their phone numbers on a 'Do Not Call' list; people turn off and go fix a snack when TV ads come on during their favorite TV show. Half of all direct mail that comes to your home is unopened, and people who find ads coming up on their favorite website actually opt-out once the ads come up. (Watch out Facebook).

One of my consultants told me marketing, as we know it, would be obsolete in 10 years; I suggested two years was more to the point. As it turned out I was right.

Who has a Yellow Page ad, a printed brochure or a flyer? We now have QR codes on the back of a business card pulling us to a hot website or PDF of a brochure, because the old ways of getting your attention is gone. Mind you I have a plumber friend who pays $9000 a month for a double page Yellow Page ad, pays $4000/month for a TV spot and has trucks loaded with advertising. He won't change because these tools have been in place so long people actually find it a convenient way to find his services.

Inbound vs. Outbound

Inbound Marketers base their success on loyalty and do so after gaining your trust. I collect emails as an opt-in practice by giving people a free eBook about Social Media Networking, having had over 200,000 followers on Twitter I know a little about that. Now mix in videos (which any fool can make and edit in minutes on their net book), blogs, pod casts, info-graphics and white papers and everyone has become an expert in a given field. Read Millionaire Messenger by Brendan Burchard for further information.

It's all about content, CRM, Social media, engagement. If you give people something interesting in any of the pull marketing strategies people will be more apt to buy from you. Don't forget about all those friends and others who see your marketing piece and send it out to their associates and their own friends. I have well over 4000 people following me on LinkedIn who have a combined influence of over 23 million followers, on Twitter my influence is over 50 million.

Unlike Vegas, where everything done in Vegas stays in Vegas, everything you say and do on the Internet stays on it forever. Your marketing efforts do as well and a good idea will go viral. I sometimes get a little overwhelmed on the Internet when it comes to the newest and best marketing methods. I'd suggest to you that adding one strategy at a time and getting good at it before adding another strategy might be the best way to enter social media marketing. Don't let it intimidate you!

Now that you obviously understand all the nuances of traditional marketing and inbound versus outbound marketing you will also understand that the next step is to realize that the future of marketing is inbound marketing. Let's explore that a little further.

It's not hard to see the Internet as a two-way street, you engage with people and they respond like a conversation. Traditional methods of marketing are rarely effective on the Internet. I used to be an innovative marketing guy, I used to be a lot of things a few years ago, but in today's fast and immediate Internet world traditional marketing is out the window.

Inbound Marketing (Pull Marketing)

We live in a world of information abundance and attention scarcity – and the amount of information creation is accelerating. 90% of the data in the world today has been created in the last two years alone. You may have heard the term content is king? That's in reference to the demand consumers put on people like us giving information to the masses. The more we create the more they want. IT makes you wonder if anyone has time to read a book or a Kindle.

Consumers are very empowered and expectant. The web provides them with instant information gratification and they expect to find whatever they want on the internet from what Michelle was wearing at the White House gala t o the location of Planet X in the solar system. They can access detailed specs, pricing, and reviews about goods and services 24/7 with a few flicks of their thumbs. Meanwhile, social media encourages consumers to share and compare, while mobile devices add a wherever/whenever dimension to every aspect of the experience.

> *"Inbound Marketing is so powerful because you have the power to give the searcher/consumer exactly what answers they are looking for at the precise point that they need it. That builds trust,*

reputation, and authority in whatever niche you are practicing this form of marketing in."

- Joshua Gill, Inbound & SEO Marketing Consultant

"Although it varies greatly with product complexity and market maturity, today's buyers might be anywhere from two-thirds to 90% of the way through their journey before they will engage with a vendor's sales rep."

- Forrester Research

1. Customers are interactive between yourself and them.
2. The Mission of most companies is now geared to the customer not the company
3. Customer engagement is on a one to one level not mass advertising and is based on behavioral psychometrics.
4. The tactics we use are continuous relationships and exploding integrated channels.
5. Marketers provide more benefits and value to the prospective customer because there is so much free stuff out there on the net. They almost need to keep people engaged, educated and entertained.
6. Prospective customers come to you through referrals, affiliates and search engines.

7. Some of the tools you are already familiar with are Inbound marketing. Content marketing, SEO, events, blogs, podcasts are designed to enhance your brand by giving your prospective clients something to listen to you.
8. Inbound marketing earns the attention of consumers and makes your company easier to find.
9. Measurements are from fact-based decisions.

Why You Need Inbound Marketing

1. It puts all the power into the hands of the consumer not the seller
2. Allows customers to interact with you when they need you 24/7. Connecting to a customer immediately when they need you and having you solve their problem is a huge win-win for everyone.
3. Inbound fuels search engine optimization results that in-turn fuels it's own system by interpreting more information to help you
4. It allows you as the marketer to shape the way your brand is perceived more accurately and thereby influencing future purchases. Have you been on a

website looking at a watch and for the next ten days you see ads from the same watch company popping up everywhere? That's programmatic advertising based on your behavior on a website – very effective!

5. You can generate better and more qualified leads for less money than the traditional method of marketing.

6. Unlike outbound marketing where you read the flyer and drop it in your waste paper basket, inbound material builds upon itself over time and continues to be viable.

How Can You Use the Benefits of Inbound Marketing?

1. Develop a persona for your perfect customer and get to know them inside out.

2. Specifically target the research you got form number 1- that's obvious!

3. Determine your unique story, in marketing terms it's called the Unique Selling Proposition (USP). Once you know that you can tell your customer why they should buy from you by designing the right content materials and letting them make the decision.

4. Are you going to use your website, email, podcast, blog Twitter, Facebook, etc. to reach your customer? Your persona that you developed on your target market will help you identify the best platform to suit them.

5. Develop a simple spreadsheet with when and how you are going to implement your plan. This helps you create and monitor the content you have given out to the various platforms to keep it 'fresh'. A good way to think about content if you need to be able to reuse it, is to develop 'ageless' content that is relevant no matter if it was written ten years ago or today. We call it 'evergreen' content. Using this approach you can get more rotation on your content by posting or tweeting the sale content numerous times over several weeks, waiting for a couple of months then re-issuing it.

Raise Your Game, Entrepreneurs

The time to experiment with Social Media is past, it is not going away and if your business is not heavily involved in a Social Media campaign you will lose to your competition. I realize Outbound marketing is still in place mainly in large organizations. Smaller more nimble businesses have realized that free or nearly free guerrilla marketing fits their budget.

The large billboards will still try to catch your eye as you drive down the roads of America and newspapers (until they finally go digital) will still have ads. Roofing companies will still send you those glossy flyers trying to sell you a $20,000 roof but it will probably say "Made from Recycled Materials" probably on the advice of their printer. Their still is relevance to use outbound tools but it's just not as complelling anymore as a method to sell when you see everyone on planes, trains and automobiles with a Smartphone in their face.

Large corporations are now devoting a significant budget in terms of human resources and money to making the most of their brand with social media and getting rid of their expenses and out-dated advertising campaigns. They realize that even though they may be partially stuck in the outbound campaign trail they need other way to generate leads to augment their established sales cycle methods.

Social Media is inexpensive, relevant, and easy to implement. The barrier to entry no longer exists. Your social media must cover the following four objectives.

1. **Positioning.** Synchronize your objectives, both business and social.

2. **Outcome** Maximize results by allocating social media where and when it makes sense in your marketing plan.

3. **Systems Integration.** Create a system that makes all your actions run smoothly

4. **Client Engagement.** Strengthen the core of your social media success rather than being left behind by the competition.

There is still a need, maybe more so, for the human connection and the following will give you some insight into handling and managing the art of personal networking one on one.

Since Social media is becoming the norm it takes us away from direct contact with those who we really want to impact – new customers. While Social media reaches so many more people there is nothing like grasping the hand of a new contact, looking him in the eye and making a connection.

When HubSpot was created a few years ago, it was founded to help businesses do inbound marketing. Rather than spending most of their marketing budget on outbound marketing tactics - like telemarketing, direct mail, email, banner ads and traditional ads like TV, radio, newspaper and magazine ads - inbound marketers attract visitors, convert visitors to leads and sales, and analyze data to identify ways to increase traffic, leads and sales over time. Businesses that have figured out how to use the Internet to "get found" by potential customers and then convert them to customers, are shifting their marketing budgets to inbound away from traditional advertising. **This shift is taking a big toll on traditional media companies.**

Digital transformation is in full swing, and companies are doing their best either to stay one step ahead, or at least to keep up with the crowd. What are some of the biggest challenges and opportunities in digital business today?

Challenges

1. Meeting Expectations of Customers in the Digital Age

The mobile, always-on generation expects very different experiences from companies and organizations, including public administration. According to a recent Harris Poll, 82% of US corporate executives said that customers' expectations of their company were "somewhat" (47%) or "much" (35%) higher than they were three years ago. Nobody wants to wait in line for services anymore. Instead, they want to be able to arrange their whole lives online.

2. Finding and Keeping the People Who Can Digitally Transform a Company

Somebody needs to build all these great user experiences that make the difference to customers' lives. But finding and keeping these people will become increasingly difficult. Designing customer interactions is as much an art as it is a skill. The best people will naturally be drawn to companies that do interesting, cutting edge stuff. That means that companies that want digital success need to become technology companies. As Marc Andreessen said in 2011: "Software is eating the world." Well, right then it was just having a snack. Now it's a banquet.

3. Managing the Omni-Channel Reality

You cannot fight fragmentation with fragmentation. Consumer side, the fragmentation is nothing you can change: on the contrary, it will only get worse. New devices, IoT, in-car entertainment, the Apple watch, Wi-Fi on airplanes… all add together to make a fragmentation of channels. That means that companies need to standardize on the inside with a digital business platform, so they can keep track of what is happening across all these channels. But today the reality is that many companies have fragmented systems in-house, instead of a single platform to rule them all.

4. Big data

Big data is presenting companies with new opportunities to learn more about their customers, enabling them not only to personalize products and services, but also to change their product development process to reflect what people really want. However, companies are still struggling with getting consumer confidence on this issue, as many consumers are turned off by hyper-personalized offers that seem to invade their personal space.

Opportunities

1. **Digital Disruption from Within**

2. Disruption is the name of the game, with established players being constantly displaced by newcomers that are digital natives. If you can't beat them, join them at their own game. Existing companies need to disrupt themselves, like Steve Jobs did when he stopped making their best-selling iPod to introduce a newer version of it.

3. **Show-rooming**

Showrooming is a big challenge for retailers, as consumers continue to increase their online shopping, but recently, there's also been a trend towards webrooming, with people checking out items online before buying them in store. And once people actually come to shops, retailers have the opportunity to keep them there and upsell, or make them long term customers. Using the IoT and beacons provides opportunities here. Online stores can't provide the same service and knowledge staff as bricks and mortar stores, and that's where businesses can build consumer engagement.

4. Digital Workforces and New Ways of Working

Startups these days can work with very small in-house teams, yet still take on the big boys by using the web and technology to create teams per project. This way of working can be very fulfilling because employees are not stuck in a company, but work only on projects they care about, and where their passion makes a huge difference to the outcome. In a world where less than 1 in 7 people are engaged at work, this could spell the end of multinational corporations as we know them.

5. The Internet of Things (IoT)

Using beacons and oculus solutions to improve customer experiences. The IoT is connecting people and devices with each other in an unprecedented way, creating rich possibilities for consumer engagement. Timing is the key element here; if you're too early you could fail, and if you're too late, you may lose your place in your industry, and ultimately fail. Companies need to consider how using connected devices can provide more value to customers and more savings for them.

6. MicroMoments

Consumers nowadays want everything here and right now, and with the power of their mobiles, it's easy for them to get what they want. Micromoments are when you are humming a tune you can't get out of your head and stop what you are doing to Google a key phrase in the song so you will know the title – absurd but I do it too!

Google recently urged bricks and mortar shops to invest more effort on micro moments, when consumers think 'I want to go.' According to Google, there's been an explosion in people conducting 'near me' searches. Even more interestingly, 50% of consumers who carry out a local search on their Smartphone visit a shop within a day, and nearly 1 in 5 of those searches lead to a purchase within a day. Businesses need to exploit these micro moments across channels. I've often done micro searches or are they geo searches? I'm in a mall and instead of walking 100 feet to the mall directory I Google the name of the mall to see what is close to me.

Now if you own a store your new best friend better be a stellar SEO guy!

Now you have the tools, explore the power (and avoid the horrors).

Up next, more stories!

Chapter 12 – The Power of Social Media (& Social Media Horror Stories)

So I have told you about social media in terms of marketing, CRM, sales, best practices, and others but it's important to know the side benefits of social media, that being **power**. I don't know about you but I hate injustice, people taking advantage of others, and for me I hate bad service in restaurants, poor quality products and politicians who lie and cheat. So I do something about it. It does work both ways fortunately. In other words, you can shame a business using social media into changing policy, taking back products, altering services, etc., but it also works for the business. A proactive business will quickly learn that they can make substantive changes to policy, customer service issues etc.

by embracing social media as their friend and keeping on top of it so social marketers like me don't catch them unawares.

After working on changing Canadian Law with Bill C-470 making the finances of charities transparent I realized "one person can make a difference". Gone are the days when people were run roughshod over by business, politicians and the like, we can complain and the more followers you have and the more you are engaged in social media the louder that voice is heard.

Three years I was at a hotel in Toronto for a week with my family. I gave a credit card with a small limit telling them that I would settle the bill with my Debit card. Every day they called my room to ask if I still intended to pay with the credit card and every day I told them no I would pay with cash. Finally, on my last day the front desk called me at 8am and demanded I come downstairs to the Front Desk to pay my bill. When I hung up on them they came to my door – what? I was not impressed.

I went downstairs, paid my bill in cash, tore a strip off the Desk Clerk and grumbled all the way to the airport.

On my flight home I wrote a blog post followed by several uncomplimentary tweets. I remember the day I sent the tweets out was November 10 because the next day was a holiday. At 10am on the holiday I received a phone call from the President of the largest hotel chain in Canada. Very apologetic, he explained my credit card raised a flag because my hotel stay exceeded the limit on my card. He apologized profusely. Then he offered me a suite for free the next time I returned to Toronto. He asked my advice on customer service as well as asking me if I would work with them on social media. The largest high-end hotel chain in Canada had 78 followers on Twitter compared to my 200,000 at the time. Someone in his IT department were monitoring their social media by following #hashtag trends yet they only had 78 people interested enough to follow them. When you looked at their 12 tweets four months out of date the reason was clear. It was obvious the social media guru watching the Internet for references to the hotel had no interest in their Twitter account.

I tweeted after the conversation to my following that the hotel had addressed the situation and I was satisfied. I never did take him up on his offer - I didn't like the hotel anyway. If you call someone out on social media and they respond with appropriate action you must give them acknowledgment otherwise you are a bully. It is only fair. The problem is that people had already seen my mini 'rants' and may not have seen the Tweet about his apology. You know what they say in the newspaper business; ruin a person's reputation on page one then retract it, in smaller type on page twenty.

My son, a young man new to Vancouver and a new job had a dream of a new sports car. It was beautiful, fast and had his name on it even the price was right so he asked me to go to the car dealership with him to 'negotiate' the price. I knew he could afford it and he deserved it so off we went to a well-known Vancouver dealership.

I was jealous from the get go, it was new and my Mustang was ten years old. The salesman told us there was no problem with a loan for the car, that he would do the paperwork meaning finding a lender and that we could pick it up the following Friday unless we heard from him to the contrary. Off we went celebrating the fact the two of us would be roaring down the highway next week in his new sports car.

Friday came and I called my fav insurance guy to join my son, wife and me there as we picked up his car. I felt a sense of doom as we pulled into the parking lot and saw the salesman duck into the bathroom. Not a good sign! You guessed it the del fell through and he 'forgot' to call my son. Bad move! I didn't lose my temper I just grumbled all the way home.

You know what I did, don't you. I wrote a blistering set of

Tweets about the 'ordeal' at 7pm on a Friday night. Saturday morning I started getting calls at 10am that I ignored. By noon my son started getting calls and brought the phone to me. The caller was the GM of the dealership telling me he hear of the situation last night and wanted to know the story. He fired the gutless salesman, as a matter of course, Friday night when he saw my Tweets. He asked what I wanted? Nothing but consideration!

He gave me the explanation, not long enough in Vancouver and not long enough in the job caused the credit to fail. Fair enough but, if only the salesman had been honest, but I guess he paid the price. I thanked the GM and he said he would personally consider another application after a few more months of employment. That was enough for me so I went to my computer and told my 'peep's, as the younger people say, that I was satisfied. The GM had given me the reasons, offered a solution and was pleasant.

He also sent me a $100 gift certificate to my favorite restaurant the next day by courier - with another apology. I love this guy and respect his business-sense. Of course, I will go back there for my next car.

No I won't tell you the name of the company suffice to say the car was not out of his affordability factor and the matter was resolved to my satisfaction.

A different situation happened at the large Canadian restaurant chain, Boston Pizza in my neighborhood. Three times in a row when my deliveries came to my home there was something missing from the order. When food is involved I get incensed but my wife loves Boston's pizza. Calling twice, me going to the pizza place to pick up the missing items did not amuse me and I vented on the Internet. A manager called the next day and offered me a $10 gift certificate. What the heck, I took it but it was only good for two weeks. With such a huge company they didn't get it. You guessed it, I never went back and told the world about their service. My wife will have to live with the disappointment. Yikes!!

I was tweeting in my fav pub (yes another drinking establishment) with pictures about the great food and how I enjoyed going there. It is so cool, the Great Bear Pub, that I go there to write. I know, imagine a guy who can write in chaos. When my bill came the manager had written across it 'Thanks, no charge and enjoy your day" Wow, it's nice to be appreciated from both customer and client. A nice cash tip to the waitress finished it off. It says a lot about a company that can monitor what is said about them both good and bad and be able to act immediately.

With a large following it is also nice to 'pay it forward'. I can afford to ReTweet a charity campaign or support a kickstarter with a good cause. It is so satisfying to give away something that you take for granted that is so welcomed by others who need help.

Bullies, malcontents, trolls and other people who use social media to spout anger and hatred drive me crazy. A national TV commentator noted today that when he reads his Twitter feed in the morning he will know what kind of day it will be by number of the hate filled tweets he reads. When I get hate mail, I take it in, suffer a moment of a hissy fit then mellow out and respond in a non threatening way, just like they tell you to do when you encounter a cougar on a trail, eyes to the ground and move slowly.

A case in point; the US dentist, Dr. Walt Palmer, DDS, who shot the old African lion in a protected sanctuary park in Africa. The story went viral to every news outlet in the world and social media had a field day vilifying him. The pictures didn't help. He had to take threw months off work and was tracked himself by people who were ready to kill him, if you believed their tweets. People need to be responsible and take a breathe before ruining someone's life.

The bottom line is that social media can make change

happen in a variety of ways. Business and personal lives have been changed forever but the benefits rely on not only the method you use but also your intent.

> *"The new source of power is not money in the hands of a few, but information in the hands of many."*
>
>
>
> **John Naisbitt**
> Expert In Future Studies

Chapter 13 – A Twitter Social Media Case Study

An International Piano Company Campaign

A Vancouver retailer and national distributor of the top rated band of pianos in the world approached me with a simple question – could I get his best quality brand piano exposure to a certain market? Not precisely sales but simply exposure.

A bit different than working with my other two large clients, PayPal and Microsoft but I told him it sounded like fun as long as he liked the way I managed campaigns. My charge per Tweet rate is $200US (+ $200/hour if travel is required) but this campaign needed a lot of tweets – I'd make sure he'd get what he wanted at a deal.

This was going to be a non-campaign campaign. I wanted to be able to approach my Twitter followers (500,000+) specifically, without feeling like I was trying to sell them something. I wanted it to be informative but from a personal level – me directly engaging them.

I met the owner of Showcase Pianos at the launch of a new Rolls at the Vancouver Rolls Royce dealership. Showcase had one of the brand's grand pianos in the lobby of the dealership (or does Rolls call their stores another name?) with a pianist playing.

This piano was not only an awesome full size grand piano but it had a magnificent lacquered black gloss. It also had a pedigree. It was played by jazz giant Herbie Hancock at a local concert and he signed it as well. It was also signed by another jazz great Chick Corea right below Herbie's. The third tidbit I got from Manuel the storeowner was that it had been the prop in the Hollywood movie, "Fifty Shades of Grey". When I told a friend about it, he asked me if I had washed my hands after playing it because of the movie's plot, lol. The price was a cool $280,000 (used).

With the storyline idea firmly settled, Manuel, asked to start the campaign by Tweeting from the Rolls shop. Hmm, this didn't settle well with me because nobody I know would ever believe that I would be at a Rolls Royce launch of a $485k automobile; it's not my style. Manuel is doing well as evidenced by his Bentley ride.

But I did have a plan. I asked him if any other high –end stores had the Fazioli brand in Vancouver. We met the next day at a store on Vancouver's Coal Harbour waterfront that was dripping money in it elegant storefront selling high-end furniture. The Fazioli piano was sitting next to the window in a display living room suite itching to be played.

These Fazioli's are works of art made of the finest materials, designed by a master pianist who is also an engineer and the finish of layer upon layer of lacquer. My client told me that a lot of people buy them as furniture not to be played. Sounds extravagant but some people just want the wow factor for their friends to admire.

My campaign had just begun. I started the campaign off on Facebook so I had more characters to setup the story. It ran like this on Facebook that I then shared on Twitter:

"Was walking d/t Vancouver & saw this incredible piano #Fazioli in a very hi-end store, phew unbelievable look to it, anyone seen it before? + pic (sent from FB to twitter May 26)"

I followed up the next from Twitter with this Tweet:

"I had to check out the #Fazioli piano close up, apparently they are the #1 #piano mfgr in the world + pic (sent from Twitter May 27)"

The plot thickened when I tweeted out that it looked so cool I'd have to try it out then I threw in a couple of proprietary features for interest.

Three days later, a piano teacher in the US tweeted me

"@garybizzo Wow, Gary, that is super cool. How does it compare in the touch of the keys to a regular piano stroke, compared to keyboards? (May 30 Twitter)."

Now I had engaged people to help me promote the campaign. Since she had approached me I fired several tweets off to her with cool technical information I got from the factory in Italy. I also told her that New York City's famous music school Juilliard has replaced all their Steinways with Fazioli's.

I got the teacher excited when I told her it had 3 pedals in the basic model and had an option for a fourth pedal. To be honest I don't really know what those pedals would even do but enclosed a very cool demo of the piano in action. She was hooked!

In the next tweet I told I would go to the store and check out the models for her because I was so enamored by these pianos and I included another link to the store.

I had pictures taken of me 'playing the $240k piano and sent her a Tweet then told her about the piano to beat all pianos, a 24k gold leaf beauty in Showcase's main showroom at a mind-blowing $585,000. Of course when I got there I shot a great pic of the storefront and tweeted that out to the world and once inside got a shot me playing that piano. You guessed it – I fired it off to her and the world.

My story was not only making sense but it was fun to learn piano facts, noodle on the pianos and tell people about them. Hmm, now what would I do for Tweets?

I decided to take pics of ShowcasePiano's manager and piano teacher introducing her in my Tweets and asking about piano LESSONS. After being a very poor duffer I needed lessons to be able rationalize the ¼ mil for one of her pianos.

Lessons, again hmm, would she play me a tune so I could tell she knew what she was doing?

"@RussellsRiff the mgr of the store www.showcasepianos.com/ played Mozart on the #Fazioli

I tried a jazz riff *(Twitter, June 15)"*

I decided to expand my story to the places in the world this piano was being played professionally and included videos. Then, of course, I took my followers on a trip to the factory outside Rome.

This was turning into an educational experience and I was having fun!

Then more people came on board to help me promote Fazioli on Twitter. I got into a great Twitter chat with a guy from Vancouver who told me about the luxury model he loved after seeing the online piano brochure I had posted.

The campaign was spread over 21 days, when I posted a new Tweet it was posted at 7am, 11am, 3pm and 7pm then I would cross-promote it to other platforms like Facebook and even LinkedIn and it was natural for my Instagram account.

My client had given me carte blanche because he loved the concept and I kept him up to date on my progress every week but I think he was bit overwhelmed when he got my invoice.

We could have done it differently, being proactive and throwing soft and hard sells, offering discounts or leasing arrangement. I even could have promoted my artist brother, David Bizzo, who is internationally-know for painting semi-realism pianos <u>but</u> I wanted to be a storyteller. I wanted to engage others to get the word out which did but would have never happened if I was doing a sales job. As it turned out one of the tweets was my most retweeted Tweet for that month. It had grown organically and there wasn't any deception.

Gary C. Bizzo @garybizzo · 26 Dec 2016
Biz playing the #Fazioli **piano** ($375,000) that was played by Herbie Hancock and was featured in the movie "50 Shades of Gray"

We certainly reached a vast number of people and with my demographic of followers specifically targeted, I gave him a lot of imprints in his target market - Canada.

The moral is, if you keep going with a targeted interesting and relevant story, good things will come.

> *"If you're passionate about something
> and you work hard,
> then I think you will be successful."*
>
>
>
> **Pierre Omidyar**
> Ebay founder

Chapter 14 – Conclusion

I used to own and operate a boutique, advertising agency back in the 1990's. Advertising and marketing comprised a whole different mind and skillset back then. A marketing professional knew how to utilize everything from business cards, newsletters, flyers, catalogs and point of sale materials to aid a business in creating a robust marketing campaign. These campaigns would cost in the tens of 1000's of dollars to implement and the conversion rate would be about 2-3% sales conversion per campaign.

Fast forward to 2017 and all this advertising material, known as collateral marketing tools, have disappeared and professional marketers like me and others had to adapt or die. I remember talking to a marketing professor at a local university who used to contract to me. He told me in a conversation in 2010 that marketing, as we know it would be dead in ten years. I laughed and said it would be within the year. I was right; but knowing that it was changing drastically allowed me to adapt faster and be on the 'leading edge' of new marketing tools and techniques.

The issue facing marketers had many facets. These are the big ones:

1. The big budgets became a thing of the past since email, social media and digital ads replaced paper and billboards. The honest truth is I used make piles of money off my clients by placing ads in magazine, flyers and those billboards. I wonder what they did with those big budgets?

2. We as marketers, had to face the problems of changing the paradigm from outbound marketing to inbound marketing. According to Wikipedia, "**Inbound marketing** is a technique for drawing customers to products and services via content marketing, social media marketing and search engine optimization." **Outbound marketing**, on the other hand, is just another name for "traditional advertising methods", it is devised to contrast with the **inbound marketing**. It

includes television and radio advertising, print advertising, telemarketing, direct mail, and outdoor advertising.

Many business people business owner who spent the last five years working extra hard, and spending scarce marketing dollars, to achieve results from traditional media - primarily direct mail, telemarketing and directories are now realizing often too late that inbound marketing is the direction they should have taken 5 years ago. I'm not sure why some companies failed to see the trends when they were being obvious.

3. Lack of Warm leads. Trends indicate that local media's projected ad growth will come from brand new business in 2017. The problem is sales reps are chasing existing dollars in their markets. Since most local media companies don't have a dedicated marketing or sales person helping to generate new, high quality leads, sales reps are left with one option to drum up new business -- cold calling. If you're in the business, you know that scribbling down that new advertiser you see in the newspaper or on a billboard and calling them up, is getting less and less effective these days. Sales leaders are now relying on their

company's website and its content to capture new customers meaning SEO is king.

4. Inconsistent Customer Revenue. Not only are sales teams constantly chasing existing advertisers, they're constantly chasing the same sales too. Inconsistent ratings, circulation numbers and viewership make insertion orders commonplace and annual buys few and far between. **Forecasting** revenue with a larger and growing portion of one-time-buys is nearly impossible. Worse still, media companies know marketing dollars are being spent elsewhere in the market... But, they haven't figured out how to capture a larger portion of their client's marketing budgets.

5. Consumers are becoming immune to traditional marketing methods. In our current environment, the average person is exposed to approximately 5,000 ads a day between Internet, mobile, television, radio, print, out of home and social media advertising. I think that a person is more likely to survive a plane crash than click on a website banner ad. With the proliferation of devices and the explosion in new advertising channels - such as native, in-app, and push advertising - there is

"Lucky Orange" 4 Engaging customers?

even steeper competition for eyeballs, along with much higher stakes to engage and convert consumers.

All this means that while content remains king, context becomes key. Blanket broadcasts and 'spray and pray' marketing tactics don't work like they used to. At best they don't deliver high ROI. At worst, ham-fisted marketing can actively harm the reputation of a brand.

Experienced marketers know in order to effectively engage consumers (whether to subscribe them, produce purchase intent, or simply increase brand awareness) they need to address the right consumer, at the right moment, through the right channel.

So how do marketers make their voice heard over the digital noise? The answer is engagement. A little program app called Lucky Orange allows you to chat with customers who have been online for a short period of time. It's very handy because you can assign someone to monitor it in your business and when someone enters the site for lets say 20 seconds a window pops up on your computer screen as well as the possible customer. They can ask you questions in real time and you can respond in like manner. It is more than an engagement tool it shows the 'prospective' customer you are on the ball!

The bottom line with your social media whether it's a campaign for a client or your own way to boost your profile and sales – enjoy yourself! Since I have identified my social media 'work' as an avocation I can get away with a lot in terms of psyching myself into putting time into because essentially it has become an exciting 'hobby.

So far I have not lost the passion I have for social media as I did for my photography business. As long as I can keep abreast of new changes, engage with cool and wonderful people I will be happy plugging away and telling all who listen how to get the results I get.

Stay Engaged!

Do You Know About Gary's Other Book?

Find **How to Start a Successful Business the First Time** on Amazon

Appendix

6-Step Social Media Checklist For Everyone

1. **Goal Setting**
   Determine what you want from your social media
   a. Are you selling an app or a product?
   b. Trying to promote a video you have produced on YouTube for your business?
   c. Use Inbound marketing to get more web traffic to enhance your profile in the world
   d. Promote a blog you are particularly proud of
   e. Do you like my favorite word – ENGAGEMENT?

2. **Your Social Audit**
   This is a classic approach for whatever kind of marketing you want to do and is really common-sense.
   a. Who is Your target audience? Create a persona for your perfect client so you are not wasting time on the wrong targets.
   b. Who are the people engaging with you? Can the audience be identified?
   c. What are your strengths and weaknesses? If you hate writing perhaps a blog is not the right place to start; consider Twitter
   d. What time or day works for you? Will you be able to reach your target audience?
   e. How much time can you afford to spend on social media?
   f. Can you afford to place ads on Facebook?

3. **Your Preferred or Needed Platforms**

   Some platforms like Twitter might appeal to you more than a blog or you may feel more engaged with friends on Facebook. This is what works for you
   a. Select as many platforms that you can adequately devote some time to
   b. What platform will appeal to your perfect customer or audience?
   c. Do you need to combine social platforms? I often Tweet then post it on LinkedIn and Facebook to get more bang for my buck.
   d. Don't get onto too many at the expense of your favorite or most effective platform for your audience.

4. **Create Your Content Strategy**

   This is particularly important in terms of how you relate to people as just followers or potential customers, e.g. you might share stuff on Facebook you would never let a prospective customer you. Consider this carefully!
   a. What type of post will work for your client and your personality so you can be genuine and get your point across, e.g. humor, politics, serious or factual.
   b. What social networks work best for your content that you want to get out there?
   c. Can you allocate money and a budget to promoting your content, e.g. Google ads, Facebook?
   d. Can you develop A/B tests to se what ads and content works better than others? Unsure of what an A/B test is? Look it up!

5. **Analytics**
   This is a must and is so simple. You need to monitor and track your platform hits. It's easy on Twitter they have analytics attached right to your profile. On Wordpress or your blog you can add Google Analytics to it for free.
   a. How is your content performing? Twitter analytics will tell you what Tweets worked and what didn't
   b. Us the relevant tools to get what you need. The freebies are fine but for more in-depth pay for a decent analytic tool.
   c. Whatever you have found to be working, don't try to be clever- replicate it!

6. **Adjust, Adjust and Engage**
   Most people will not get it right the first time. Your goal here is to see what works through results and analytics and compare them on a regular basis to know what to change and when
   a. Use the analytic tools routinely and do a comprehensive analysis of what needs adjusting – it will usually be obvious. I've made little changes that doubled sales from one day to the next.
   b. Measure your data and compare it to your defined goals in #1 to keep on track.

Social Media Tools for Business

Some of these links may no longer be in service or have changed names, but do make a Google search to find out what tool has replaced it OR go to my website GaryBizzo.com

#BePresent https://mustbepresent.com/

Adobe Spark https://spark.adobe.com/

Audiense https://audiense.com

BeFunky https://www.befunky.com/

Bitly https://bitly.com/

Brandgauge http://www.brandgauge.com/

Buffer http://bufferapp.com/

Buzz Sumo http://buzzsumo.com/

Canva https://www.canva.com/

CardMunch

https://www.evernote.com/cardmunch/Welcome.action

Click to Tweet https://clicktotweet.com/

Commun.it http://commun.it/quick_actions

Compfight http://compfight.com/

CoSchedule http://coschedule.com/

CrowdBooster http://CrowdBooster.com

Crowdfire http://crowdfire.com

Curalate https://www.curalate.com/

dlvr.it http://dlvrit.com

Easelly https://www.easel.ly/

Edgar https://meetedgar.com/

Engage by Twitter https://blog.twitter.com/2016/introducing-twitter-engage-0

Facebook Insights https://www.facebook.com/help/search/?q=insights

Facebook Live https://live.fb.com/

Fanpage Karma http://www.fanpagekarma.com/

Fanpoint http://www.fanpoint.com/

Feedly http://feedly.com/

FiveHundredPlus http://www.fivehundredplus.com/

Flare https://filament.io/flare

Flashissue http://flashissue.com/

Followerwonk https://moz.com/followerwonk

GIPHY http://giphy.com/

Google URL Builder https://support.google.com/analytics/answer/1033867?hl=en

GroupTweet http://grouptweet.com/

Have2HaveIt https://have2have.it/

Hootsuite Hootsuite.com

Iconosquare https://pro.iconosquare.com/

IFTTT https://ifttt.com/channels

Infogr.am https://infogr.am/

Instagram for Business https://business.instagram.com/

Jelly http://jelly.co/

Keyhole http://keyhole.co/

Klear http://klear.com/

Klout http://klout.com/home

Later http://later.com/

LICEcap http://www.cockos.com/licecap/

LikeAlyzer http://likealyzer.com/

Linktotweet http://www.linktotweet.com/

Lucky Orange http://www.luckyorange.com

ManageFlitter http://manageflitter.com/

Mention https://mention.com/

Mrsocial http://www.mrsocial.me/

Must Be Present http://mustbepresent.com/

Nuvi https://www.nuvi.com/

Nuzzel http://nuzzel.com/

Pablo https://pablo.buffer.com/

Paper.li http://paper.li/

Pexels https://www.pexels.com/

Piktochart http://piktochart.com/

Pocket http://getpocket.com/a/

Post Planner http://www.postplanner.com/

Powtoon http://www.powtoon.com/

quickmeme http://www.quickmeme.com/

Quuu.co http://quuu.co/

Rapportive http://rapportive.com/

Respond https://buffer.com/respond/

Rev http://www.rev.com/

SharedCount http://www.sharedcount.com/

ShareRoot http://tools.shareroot.co

Social Rank https://www.socialrank.co/

Socialdraft http://socialdraft.com

SocialMention http://www.socialmention.com/

SocialRank https://socialrank.com/

Sprout Social http://sproutsocial.com/

SteadyDemand http://www.steadydemand.com/Google-Plus-Brand-Audit-Tool.php

Swayy http://app.swayy.co/#content

Tagboard https://www.tagboard.com/

Twazzup http://twazzup.com/

Tweepi http://www.tweepi.com/

Tweet Jukebox http://www.tweetjukebox.com/

Tweet4me http://tweet4.me/

Tweetcaster https://tweetcaster.com/

Tweetdeck https://tweetdeck.twitter.com

TweetReach http://tweetreach.com/

Tweriod http://www.tweriod.com/

Twitpress http://www.twitpress.co/

Twtrland http://twtrland.com/

Typeform https://www.typeform.com/

VideoScribe http://www.videoscribe.co

Wishpond https://www.wishpond.com/

Yotpo https://www.yotpo.com/

Zapier https://zapier.com/

About the Author

Gary "The Biz" Bizzo

Gary Bizzo has mentored over 1000 business leaders, investors and entre-preneurs. His book *How to Start a Successful Business – The First Time!* was nominated for the International *2014 Small Business Book Awards*. He was a national finalist in the 2014 *Business Development Bank of Canada Mentorship Award* and Entrepreneur Magazine said Gary Bizzo is one of "17 Masters of Marketing & PR that entrepreneurs can learn from." He was on the list of the *Top 200 Philanthropists & Social Influencers* included among Elon Musk and Melinda Gates as the Most Influential Do-Gooders in the World for 2017.

Gary Bizzo helped change Canadian Law through Bill C-470 that made charities more transparent. He is a sought after speaker, respected author and business writer for national and international magazines. As a Brand Influencer he has worked for many corporations including Microsoft, PayPal and 3M. In 2017, Forbes Magazine said he was #9 on the List of the Top 25 Business Accounts on Twitter where he has several hundred thousand followers along with LinkedIn and Facebook.

Need Help Implementing Your Social Media?

Do you have no idea how to maintain, let alone implement, the social media people tell you that you need? The reality is that if you are not engaging your customers with social media now your ship has left for rough seas. Let us do the implementation and the work for you.

We will help you determine what kind of visibility you need and what level of integration works for you and your budget. We will get you hooked up professionally to the personal **Facebook** platform, to the business **LinkedIn**, to the fast paced world of **Twitter** and more. We can take the worry out of your Social Media presence. We can offer Social Media development packages; affiliate marketing programs, social media marketing campaigns, and more. We can make you a rock star! We can provide content for your social media especially the immediacy of tweets written by a professional and maintain your online presence.

Gary and his team are committed to the concept, that social media marketing integration is successful only through the strategic marriage of substantive content and calculated strategy. Our goal is to provide SOLUTIONS and profitability. Join the Evolution!

Contact Gary
1-604-805-2025
or Email: CEO@GaryBizzo.com

Made in the USA
San Bernardino, CA
03 February 2018